Eliminate Your Retirement Gap

The Network Marketing Solution

Kathi Minsky

Requests for permission should be addressed to the author at: Global Success Team, Inc.
P.O. Box 371478 Las Vegas, NV 89137

ISBN 978-0-9893180-1-3

2nd Edition

Printed in the United States of America

Publisher: Global Success Team, Inc.

Additional books may be purchased at
www.EliminateYourGap.com

DEDICATION

I thank God for the inspiration to complete this book. It addresses a concern that has been on my heart and mind for a long time.

To Mike, my husband of 38 years who has always been there for me whatever crazy or sane idea I have decided to pursue. We both agree that Network Marketing was by far my wisest choice.

To my friends Karen and Dwayne Fontaine who pursued me until I caught them. I love you both.

To the more than 15 million people who have chosen Network Marketing as the vehicle to achieve their dreams. May you realize every one.

Here's my hope that this book will provide you the information and inspiration that it is not too late to change the course of your future. Be sure to thank the person who thought enough of you to share this idea.

I wish you every success.

Author's Note

We all understand an **INCOME GAP**. In simple terms, it is when your bank balance runs out before your bills do. It is immediate. An Income Gap cannot be ignored.

A RETIREMENT GAP is far more subtle and potentially more serious. It could negatively affect your life for 20 to 30 years. A **RETIREMENT GAP** is the **difference between** the income a person will **NEED** in retirement and the resources they will **HAVE** available when they retire.

The days when our parents received a guaranteed pension and a gold watch are over. Most of us will need to rely on work-related benefits, personal savings and Social Security in retirement. Your savings will need to last longer because people are living longer.

First, we will determine IF you have a Gap. Then, we can explore potential solutions, including Network Marketing.

It is important to establish your retirement goals while you still have time to make adjustments in your strategy. If you have reached the age of 30, you should begin planning now for your future. **Regardless of your age**, this book will provide potential action steps to maximize your personal retirement plan and "fill the gaps".

I applaud your willingness to examine your own situation and consider positive changes that could literally last a lifetime.

Thank you for allowing me the privilege to be your guide through this process.

Kathi Minsky

CONTENTS

No one can go back and start a new beginning, but anyone can start today and make a new ending.

-Maria Robinson

CHAPTER 1

LIFE CAN CHANGE IN A SINGLE DAY

I came to Network Marketing by accident ...literally!

At the age of 37, I had recently opened a commercial real estate office in my hometown of Fairbanks, Alaska. I had developed a solid client base in my apprenticeship and was optimistic about the future.

My husband and I and two friends decided to make the 360-mile trip to Anchorage over the Thanksgiving weekend to spend the holiday with family and friends. We never made it. A driver coming north from Anchorage, in a hurry to get home, crossed the double-lines coming up a hill while passing a semi-truck. We crashed head-on at a combined impact of over 110 miles per hour.

Among other injuries, I suffered the first of what would eventually total more than 50 mild to minor heart attacks over the next twelve years.

After three months in and out of the hospital, I was finally able to return to my real estate office and resume work on a limited basis.

My health continued to deteriorate year after year. I knew I would not be able to keep up the pace forever, but we simply could not meet our obligations without my income, so I persevered and created a successful commercial real estate agency.

Every appointment with the heart doctor included a stern warning that ignoring my health could not continue without consequences.

FROM $1,000,000 TO ZERO

In 1999, at the age of 49, I had just been informed by my bookkeeper that I had surpassed my goal of earning $1,000,000 in personal commissions for the year. It was only October.

I was "on top of the world" as I left for yet another appointment with the heart doctor. I delivered my monitor to the nurse and waited for the doctor to come into the examining room.

I expected him to issue his standard warning, prescribe more pills and send me on my way. The visit was far from my expectation.

My attacks were increasing in both intensity and frequency. He told me there was nothing more he could do for me if I was not willing to make changes in my work schedule and lifestyle. He recommended that I put my affairs in order because the next attack would probably be the last one.

I was devastated! It finally sunk in. "What about my husband? What about my children, and my grandchildren?" I was only 49 years old.

I went to my office straight from that appointment, put my keys on the desk of my Associate Broker and explained that I would not be returning to work. I told her to hire an attorney, draw up the papers and the business would be hers from that day forward. Needless to say, she jumped at the offer. That decision marked my final day as a real estate broker.

My dream was gone. What was I going to do?

At 49 years old, **I did not have a Retirement Gap, I had a Retirement Crater!**

3 YEARS EARLIER

My friend, Karen, had called me about a company she and her husband, Dwayne had joined. We had been friends for many years, and I trusted them both implicitly. My original concern was that someone had taken advantage of them. I cautioned them about getting involved. But, they were already making a little money and were very excited about sharing the idea with their good friends. I said, "Okay, we'll look at it".

A few days later a video cassette and some materials arrived in the mail. I set them both aside, probably never really intending to look at either of them.

My friend was delicately persistent. She would call every couple of weeks and ask, "Have you watched it yet?" Each time I would make an excuse, but continued to promise that we would watch it and get back to her.

Finally, tired of disappointing her, I said we "really will watch it within the week".

I corralled my husband, and we sat down together and put in the video cassette. Since it was only 15 minutes long, we agreed that we would watch it together, then nicely tell our friends that we looked at it, but were not interested.

We watched it once. Then we watched it again. Then we got out pen and paper and tried to figure out what was wrong with it. My husband, Mike had been in the banking profession for over 30 years, and his conservative nature knew there had to be a catch, but we could not figure it out. It seemed like we just needed to get a few customers for this phone company and find a few people who wanted to make a little money. Since we both knew people who were always open to new opportunities, we started making a list. Oh NO!

The company had been in business for seven years and offered discounted long distance service. At the time, the long distance rate in Alaska was .45 cents per minute. This company was offering the exact same service at .22 cents per minute. It seemed like a "no brainer".

I called my friend. "Okay, we cannot figure out what is wrong with this. Is there anyone in Alaska doing it?" They called the company, and found that a distributor from South Carolina was coming to Fairbanks the next week to meet with several people, and go over the business plan. I took the information and said I would get back to her after the meeting.

The next day, I was at the hairdresser and asked my friend, Maria if she had ever heard of this type of company before, and she had not.

I told her about the meeting I planned to attend. She asked if she could come with me. I said, "Sure".

Maria called the next day and said another friend who was a policeman was interested in making some money too, and could she bring him. I said, "Sure".

I did not mention it to anyone else. I still was not sure it was actually legitimate. I did not want to hurt my business reputation if it turned out that it was not.

Just before I was to leave for the meeting, I attended a Chamber of Commerce Event, and mentioned to a friend that I would be leaving early because I was going to a meeting about a part-time business that was opening in Alaska. I felt a tap on my shoulder, and a husband and wife who owned a local janitorial company asked me if they could go with me. I said, "Sure".

So, here I go with four friends to the home of a total stranger having absolutely no idea what to expect. I was happy to be accompanied by our policeman friend. Surely, he would recognize if this were not on the up and up.

Frankly, the presenter was a little "over the top" and kept turning his laser pointer on me. He was wearing a decent suit with white socks (I later found out he had come to Alaska unprepared for the winter cold, and had to borrow them). When he told us how much money he was making, I was dubious.

As he spoke about the financial potential, I remained skeptical, still trying to figure out what was wrong with this. It seemed too good to be true.

My friends, however, had no reservations and got excited. They wanted to join. WHAT did they see that I did not see? I walked out of the meeting with three applications and checks for the full amount of each sponsorship. What was I going to do, now? I had to join!

We set a meeting at my house for the next week and took what limited materials we had received from my friends (now they were my sponsors) and started gathering customers. By the end of the next week, we had sent in over 100 customer applications. Who would not want to reduce their long distance expense from .45 cents per minute to .22 cents?

I decided this might be worth a trip to Portland to attend a new distributor training. I could learn more about the company and how the business plan worked, then come back and teach it to my little team.

I flew to Portland, cautiously excited. Imagine my shock to see a small asterisk at the bottom of the training manual, "Service not available in Alaska".

I returned home to the same manila envelope that had arrived on each of my friend's doorsteps that week. ALL, but ONE application (my sister's in California) was returned with the same statement. "This service is not available in Alaska".

The next team meeting had a totally different atmosphere. Naturally everyone looked to me for answers as I had "gotten them into this". I was totally embarrassed.

Then I started thinking. We were all from different areas of the country and had relatives across the "lower 48" states who could use the service where they lived. We began calling family and friends and eventually gathered the required 20 customers, still not having the service ourselves.

Then something happened. I got a check. It was for .64 cents, for my sister's first month usage commission. I was actually excited. It had worked just as promised.

What was even more interesting was that they paid me again the next month for the work I had done the first month.

For the next three years, we continued meeting at my home on Sunday afternoons. The group grew to about 80. We spent most of our time helping people identify 20 friends and family from the "lower 48" who might want to save money on their phone bill. We still had no idea what we were supposed to be doing, but the meetings were fun, and we were being paid commissions every month on the customers we gathered. Interesting!

BACK TO 1999

The day I walked out of my real estate office, for the last time, was completely devastating. I had worked hard for 12 years to accomplish my dream career goals. They went down the drain in a single day. My income went from over $1,000,000 in 1999 to ZERO in 2000.

Except for one thing!

That little phone company deal that I had started three years earlier was still sending checks. To my surprise, the checks were actually growing each month.

Every month, a few others caught onto the idea and joined the team. Many customers, from across the country, became distributors, and I was getting paid not only on the customers I gathered, but all the customers that were being added by any team member in the organization.

Hmmmm, I thought. Maybe I could do a little more with this company. The attraction was that I could work when I wanted and rest when I needed. I was having fun with my friends, so there was no stress involved. I did not have employees, a bookkeeper, office rent, or utilities. Okay, so maybe this wasn't such a bad idea after all.

The internet was beginning to catch on, and I now had access to millions of people across the country with the click of a mouse.

The next year, I increased my income from 5-figures to 6-figures per year. I knew what to do. I just needed to "step it up". In 2001, I was able to retire my husband five years early from his banking career. **We still did not have the service in Alaska.**

Two years later, I had become #37 money earner in a company of over 2,000,000 distributors and had reached their top pay rank. That $245 investment was now looking like a pretty good deal.

In 2004, we decided it was time to move to a warmer climate. We purchased a home in Oregon, packed our belongings, and made our final trip down the Alcan Highway.

One of the most amazing things about network marketing is the true portability of your income. You can live and work from anywhere. The company simply sends your check to a different address, or in today's world, direct deposits it into any bank account you designate.

We had been in Oregon for only a few months, when a certified letter arrived from the company. They had filed Bankruptcy, and we would not be getting any further payments. **After eight years, it was over!**

THE VALUE OF A NETWORK

Initially, we were devastated. Yet, one thing became totally clear over the next few days. The business was not successful simply because of the cheap long distance rates. It was successful because of the network of people we had created relationships with over the past eight years. Even though the company was gone, those relationships were fully intact.

When that fact sinks in, you will understand network marketing at its core. The products are important. The company is important. The pay plan is important. But, ultimately, it is YOU and the network you build that create the real value. It is one more reason why people who join this profession have such diverse backgrounds and experiences. **If you already have, or are willing to build a network, you can build a future**.

I immediately connected with our top leaders. We began our search for a new network marketing company that was financially solid, with strong marketing and leadership.

We knew we needed to find products and a company that would endure over time so that we would never have to experience this loss again.

In this book, I share the process we went through to find the products, company, pay plan and sponsor who were the right fit for our team.

We examined over 70 companies based on specific criteria we had agreed would best suit our needs. It was a surprising discovery that there are **many wonderful companies** offering products and services that have exceptional stories to tell. I know you will find what you are looking for if you follow this roadmap.

Once we selected a company, we began collecting applications from throughout our established network. In the first 58 days, the team sponsored more than 1,400 new distributors. We achieved the company's HIGHEST pay level in only 3 months, which had never been done before, or since.

Everyone who participated received their first commission check the next month. Eight years later, many continue to earn significantly larger checks than they did in the previous company that had gone bankrupt.

I share this story for a reason. Yes, companies come and go over the years. It happens in the traditional business world, as well.

So, while you want to make an educated decision about the company you join, if you serve your team and stay connected, your network is the most valuable asset you bring to the table. It does not matter if your network is built of friends and neighbors, business associates or social media contacts.

If you keep your network intact, you can create an amazing life and future for you and your family throughout your career.

As a result of the decision to join the network marketing profession, I enjoy the lifestyle and benefits that most people seek in retirement. I wish that same experience for you.

Before you decide whether network marketing will help you accomplish your future goals, let's take an honest look at your current plan and discover if you are "on track" to achieve the lifestyle you dream of in retirement. If you find that you are on the right path, you can be comforted in the good decisions and planning you have made for your future.

If the Retirement Estimator reveals that, like **78% of Americans**, your plan is not fully secure, and you have a Retirement Gap, I hope you will take action to "fill the gap". The solution may be a second job, reducing your expenses and saving more, starting a small business or joining the millions who are creating additional income through network marketing.

If you start your plan early enough, you will have options.

*If you don't design your own life plan, chances are you'll fall into someone else's plan. And guess what they have planned for you? **Not much**.*

~Jim Rohn

CHAPTER 2

DO YOU HAVE A RETIREMENT GAP?

I now live in Las Vegas, Nevada in a community whose population includes many retired small business owners, government employees, and business professionals.

In the past few years, I have been saddened by the 100's of home foreclosures happening around me. Many of these good people worked 30 to 40 years in their chosen profession, to enjoy retirement, play golf and travel, but that's not the life they are living today. Many have been forced to take part-time menial jobs that are physically demanding, and not meant to be done by a 60, 70 or even 80 year old worker. Some have even been forced to move in with their children.

I was dismayed to hear the stories of unexpected or unplanned events that had quickly eroded their saving and retirement funds.

I suggested to some that they consider earning a part-time income doing what network marketers do every day; sharing products they believe in, and helping others earn additional income. Often, their reaction was similar to my own at my first exposure to network marketing. We tend to reject what we don't understand.

My goal is simple and transparent, provide information and promote understanding to help the willing. It is my sincere hope that your mind will stay open as I share the many success stories of real people who have done it. If, after reading this book, you decide that network marketing is not for you, at least you have made an informed decision.

Let's look at some facts. Then, take an honest look at your own retirement status. Whatever you do, don't wait until it is too late to make decisions that will potentially affect the last 20 to 30 years of your life.

DISTURBING STATISTICS

Kiplinger's reports that **78%** of Americans 55 or older have **under-funded** retirement strategies.

One in three Americans over 55 has LESS THAN $10,000 in their bank account.

In a recent survey completed by Wells Fargo Bank consisting of middle-class Americans, **33%** said they would have to **work until they were 80 years** old based on their current circumstances.

SOCIAL SECURITY generally accounts for 20 to 35% of post-retirement income needs.

Yet statistics show that over **50% of retirees find themselves living on Social Security EXCLUSIVELY within 10 years of retirement**.

I encourage every reader, regardless of age, to go to www.ssa.gov/myaccount. Create your personal Social Security account to receive an estimate of your potential benefits. This will be helpful in determining if you have a Retirement Gap.

GOVERNMENT STATISTICS

The average 65-year-old male will live to 83

The average 65 year old female will live to 85

You should assume you will live to 90

WHAT IF YOU BECOME ILL?

30% of people who retired **before 65** years old, did so because of health problems or a job loss, not of their own choosing. Many, like me, chose alternative options rather than continuing traditional medicine. I spent approximately $300,000 to regain my health. None of it was covered by insurance.

Fidelity Investments estimates that the average 65-year-old couple will spend $240,000 **out-of-pocket** on non-covered health care costs during their retirement.

Medicare does not typically cover expenses associated with long-term care. Worse yet, **Medicaid** is not available until AFTER you have depleted most of your life savings, including your home equity.

Nearly 2/3 of all Bankruptcies filed in the US are the direct result of overwhelming medical expenses.

79% of individuals filing bankruptcy for medical reasons actually had medical insurance in place at the time they were diagnosed, but treatment coverage was limited. Retirees are becoming a rapidly growing segment of these statistics.

I personally have a plan to stay healthy, but statistics are not in my favor, nor in yours. Have you included these contingencies in your plan?

THE TIME TO PLAN IS NOW

If you are 35 - 60 years old, you should already have your long-term retirement strategy in place.

Employee Benefit Research Institute reports that Generation X'ers are not doing much better than the Baby Boomer generation. In Gen X households, (born between 1965 and 1978), **OVER 50%** are already behind in saving for eventual retirement.

If you are 50 - 60 years old, and your strategy includes full or part time work or small business activities, you should be working that plan no less than five years before retirement while your network is still strong.

CALCULATE YOUR RETIREMENT GAP

Let me first say, I am not a financial expert. I took the best of what made simple sense to create the Retirement Estimator. I, then, ran it past a few real experts who said "That is the simplest form I have ever seen. Could I use it in my business?"

Every individual situation is different for the millions of future retirees. After you have completed this basic form, I recommend you go over it with your financial advisor to determine if you have variances that the form does not include.

Read the explanation, then fill out the ANNUAL RETIREMENT ESTIMATOR on page 19.

HOW TO USE THE RETIREMENT ESTIMATOR

Step 1, Lines 1 - 3: Figure your current Annual Income, then add a growth factor based on the number of years remaining until you actually plan to retire. This will provide your Projected Annual Income in the year of your anticipated retirement.

Step 2, Line 4: Each of us has a certain lifestyle. It costs a certain amount of money each year. The typical minimum retirement goal is 80% of your average income over the last five years of employment. Less than that and you may find yourself house-bound instead of on the golf course or visiting your grandchildren. What is your Targeted Annual Income after you retire? Enter it on line 4.

Step 3, Lines 5 - 13: Figure your Estimated Annual Retirement Income. You will typically have one or more of three sources: Pension Benefits (lines 5-7), Social Security Income (lines 8-10), Savings Accounts including 401Ks and IRAs (lines 11-13). An adjustment for each revenue stream is included, allowing for growth increases between now and retirement (if applicable).

Step 4, Line 14: Most experts agree that if you retire at 65, **you should expect to withdraw no more than 4% per year of your Retirement Savings** (line 13) based on the possibility that you may live to the age of 90.

If you plan to retire earlier, adjust that number to 3%, and if you plan to retire later, adjust it to 5%. Your financial advisor will be able to help you with your individual circumstances.

Step 5, Line 15: Estimated Annual Retirement Income from all sources (Add: Line 7 + Line 10 + Line 14)

Step 6, Line 16: Subtract, Line 15 (Annual Income from all sources) from Line 4 (Targeted Annual Retirement Income). Enter that amount on Line 16.

You will either have a surplus (congratulations, you are one of the fortunate 22%) or, if you are like 78% of the population, you have discovered your **Retirement Income Gap**.

If you want a FULL PAGE VERSION of the Retirement Estimator, or if this one is filled out, go to: www.EliminateYourGap.com to download a copy.

(Intentionally left blank so you could calculate)

	ANNUAL RETIREMENT ESTIMATOR THIS CHART IS FOR ESTIMATION PURPOSES ONLY © EliminateYourGap.com	
1	Current Annual Income Combined Monthly Household Income **x** 12	
2	Growth Factor @ 3 % per year Line 1 **x** .03 **x** _____ years until retirement	
3	Projected Annual Income at Retirement (Line 1 **+** Line 2)	
4	Targeted ANNUAL Retirement Income You might consider 80% of Line 3	
5	Projected Annual Income From Defined Benefit /Pension Plans	
6	Benefits Plan Growth Factor @ 3% per year Line 5 **x** .03 **x** _____ years until retirement	
7	Projected Annual Benefits Income (Line 5 **+** Line 6)	
8	Estimated Household Social Security (SSI) Monthly Benefits **x** 12 (www.ssa.gov)	
9	SSI Growth Factor @ 3% per year Line 8 **x** .03 **x** _____ years until retirement	
10	Projected Annual SSI Income at Retirement (Line 8 **+** Line 9)	
11	Current Retirement Savings Total 401(k), IRAs, Savings, Annuities	
12	Growth Factor @ 5% per Year Line 13 **x** .05 **x** _____ years until retirement	
13	Projected Total Retirement Savings (Line 11 **+** Line 12)	
14	Annual Savings Withdrawal Rate of 4% / Year Based on Retirement at 65 (Line 13 **x** .04)	
15	Estimated TOTAL Annual Retirement Income (Line 7 + Line 10 + Line 14)	
16	SURPLUS OR INCOME GAP (LINE 4 - LINE 15) IF LINE 16 IS MORE THAN LINE 4 = SURPLUS IF LINE 16 IS LESS THAN LINE 4 = GAP	

GOOD NEWS – BAD NEWS

Your Retirement GAP may be as little as $3,000 to $10,000 per year. However, when accumulated over time, it could have a serious impact on the quality of your life in retirement if adjustments are not made.

FILL THE GAP

EXAMPLE of how you might fill the Gap:

Let's say that your Retirement Income Gap is **$6,000 per year**.

You have TWO CHOICES if you want to get your plan back on schedule:

DECREASE YOUR MONTHLY EXPENDITURES by $500 per month ($6,000 per year) and save the difference in your retirement saving fund.

INCREASE YOUR MONTHLY INCOME by $500 per month ($6,000 per year).

The chart on the next page shows the **CASH EQUIVALENT VALUE** of any additional residual income you generate, and the effect it would have on the value of savings toward your future retirement.

Figures are shown for both monthly and annual incomes based on interest rates of 1%, 2%, 4%, or 5%.

Adding just $6,000 per year ($500.00 per month) in Residual Income at a 2% interest rate (which is high as of this writing) is the equivalent of adding $300,000 to your retirement savings account. Pretty impressive!

Residual Income Generated		Cash Value Equivalent To Money Held In CD's			
Monthly Amount	Annual Amount	1 % Rate	2 % Rate	4 % Rate	5 % Rate
$ 500	$ 6,000	$ 600,000	$ 300,000	$ 150,000	$ 120,000
$ 1,000	$ 12,000	$1,200,000	$ 600,000	$ 300,000	$ 240,000
$ 2,000	$ 24,000	$2,400,000	$1,200,000	$ 600,000	$ 480,000
$ 3,000	$ 36,000	$3,600,000	$1,800,000	$ 900,000	$ 720,000
$ 5,000	$ 60,000	$6,000,000	$3,000,000	$1,500,000	$1,200,000
$ 7,000	$ 84,000	$8,400,000	$4,200,000	$2,100,000	$1,680,000
$10,000	$120,000	$12,000,000	$6,000,000	$3,000,000	$2,400,000

What will it take to fill your Retirement Gap?

My ANNUAL Retirement Gap is $ _____.

If I create an additional $_____ per month (from Chart) at _____% (from Chart) that would be the equivalent of adding $_____ (from Chart) to my Retirement Savings Account.

Does the idea of creating a monthly residual income which could "fill the gap" make sense?

EXPECT THE UNEXPECTED

We should not leave this chapter without discussing additional issues that often surface during the course of a 20 – 30 year retirement. We don't plan them, they are simply part of life.

- A spouse or partner dies causing a partial loss of Social Security Income, and potentially the loss or reduction of pension and insurance benefits

- Uninsured or under-insured medical expenses

- 17% of adult children return home or need parental support

- Seven percent of grandparents are partially or completely raising their grandchildren

You may want to adjust your own calculations to include any or all of the above. Expecting life to be constant for 20 – 30 years left me feeling vulnerable. I decided more was better. You may want to consider the same.

That's what Kay and her son Bob did. I think their story will inspire you with possibilities.

PLAN B BECOMES PLAN A

At age 50, Kay was a busy mom of 5 children with a part-time job as the librarian at her church. Her husband was a career teacher and head of the math department of the local high school.

At the time, Kay had been experiencing some health issues with chronic pain and arthritis.

A friend recommended several products available from a network marketing company that might be helpful. Kay describes the results as a "life changing experience".

Not one to keep a good idea to herself, she began sharing her experience with others and eventually built a small part-time business.

In 1975, when Kay was 55 years old, her husband was driving one of their children from Massachusetts to Oregon to attend college when he was struck by a drunk driver and killed instantly.

Kay was left with his $480 per month retirement and a $70 per month veteran's benefit, which was not nearly enough to secure her future.

However, the part-time network marketing business she had started was generating some much needed additional income, and she decided to give it her full attention.

Two years later, her son Bob, who had just ended a job on the west coast, due to funds drying on his project, noticed that his mom was flying to Hawaii and other resort destinations and driving a new car. He knew she could not be accomplishing this on a $550 widow's pension. He wondered what was funding this change in lifestyle, and flew home to check it out.

To his surprise, his mom shared that she had built her network marketing income to over $4,500 per month, which is more than his dad had earned after 39 years as a department head in education.

Since Bob was between jobs and open to the idea, Kay invited him to join her. Working together for the past 36 years has been a rewarding endeavor for both. Their annual income now exceeds $250,000 per year.

Today at the age of 92, Kay continues to enjoy the benefits of the business they built together by creating a successful network of distributors across the country.

The business is not only a legacy to Bob, but in its third generation will become security for a special needs grandson.

BEGINNING TO SEE THE POSSIBILITIES?

Throughout this book, you will hear stories of ordinary people who ran out of traditional options and turned to network marketing. What I love most about them is they are not all "headliners" at big events. Most are everyday people who worked hard, followed a plan and are living the dream that many never achieve; a comfortable, financially secure retirement, on their own terms.

Isn't that what we are all seeking?

You are where you are TODAY in your life because of decisions you made 5 years ago.

Where you will be in 5 years, will be determined by decisions you make today.

Next, we will explore the truth about making money. There are, arguably, only four basic ways to generate income. If you have a Retirement Gap, you will need to decide on one of them, or make major lifestyle changes in order to accommodate your future reduced income.

Let others lead small lives, but not you. Let others argue over small things, but not you. Let others cry over small hurts, but not you. Let others leave their future in someone else's hands, but not you.

~Jim Rohn

CHAPTER 3

THE FOUR WAYS TO CREATE INCOME

Now that you have identified your Retirement Income Gap let's look at some potential ways to eliminate it.

There are only two options:

DECREASE your expenses

INCREASE your income or savings

If you are five years or more from retirement, and have determined that you have a Retirement Gap, you could consider:

- Saving more of what you currently earn
- Plan to work additional years
- Cut back on spending
- Downsize your lifestyle (home, etc.)
- Get a second job.
- Start a part-time traditional business
- Build a network marketing business

If, like many people, your budget is already stretched to the limit, and you have trimmed your expenses as much as reasonably possible, you may need to consider additional sources of revenue.

FOUR WAYS TO CREATE INCOME

Here are the four basic ways to create income:

- Be an Employee – Blue or White Collar

- Own a Small Business

- Own a Big Business

- Become an Investor

Every income source falls into one of these four categories.

Bestselling Author, Robert Kiyosaki has written numerous books and articles on this subject. If you wish to go into more depth, you will find some of his titles in the Appendix.

The Chart on page 27 shows a comparison of the four ways you can create wealth, with the addition of the network marketing business model. **Notice that network marketing combines the best features of each.** You may begin to see why 15 million people have turned to this idea.

We will provide a brief overview of the four ways to create income. You decide what options make sense given your individual circumstance.

	EMPLOYEE	SELF-EMPLOYED SMALL BUSINESS	NETWORK MARKETING	BIG BUSINESS	INVESTOR
DESCRIPTION	White Collar Blue Collar	Own Your Job	Independent Distributor	Own A System or Large Franchise	Real Estate Investor Large Business Stocks, Etc.
HOW MONEY IS EARNED	Trade Time For Money	Independent Sales Professionals Small Business	Part-Time Full-Time	Own A System That Works FOR YOU	Passive Income
STOP WORKING	Income Stops	Income Stops	Residual Continues	Income Continues	Generally No Effect
RISK	0	Start-up Costs	Small Start-up Fee	Large Investment	Large Investment
POTENTIAL	Limited by Time	Limited by Time	Unlimited	Unlimited	Unlimited
ISSUES	Build Someone Else's Dream	Employees Stress / Overhead	Learn Some New Skills	Start up Costs	Need $$$ to start
NEGATIVES / POSITIVES	NO Freedom NO Leverage	NO Freedom NO Leverage	Freedom Leverage	Freedom Leverage	Freedom Leverage

1. EMPLOYEE – SOMEONE ELSE'S DREAM

You may have a job currently, or you may be searching for your next career, but once you have reached retirement age, the options narrow and often the pay scale and benefits decrease.

You may say, "I am more dependable, I will work harder, I have more knowledge". Unfortunately, that has not been the most effective argument in this new Performance Economy.

Most financial experts recommend that if you plan to have a job or small business after retirement, you need to begin preparations at least five years in advance of your anticipated retirement date while your skills are fresh and your network is still intact.

Here's the real problem with getting another job. **You have to keep doing it to get paid.** Each of us only has 24 hours in a day. You need to sleep and hopefully have time left over for family and friends.

THE LEVERAGE PROBLEM

What is leverage? The Business Dictionary defines it as: *The ability to multiply the outcome of one's efforts without a corresponding increase in the consumption of resources* (namely you).

When you work a 40-50 hour work week, it is about all you will physically be able to do as you age. The heart is often willing, the body is not quite as cooperative as it once was.

As an employee, you rely completely on your own efforts. You typically have no leverage to create additional income within the scope of your employment.

That is because **your company owner is the one with the leverage, not you**.

If it is difficult for you to let go of the employee mentality, I suggest you recognize it and settle on the best option in that category which will bridge your gap.

2. SMALL BUSINESS – OWN YOUR JOB

If your full-time occupation lends itself to becoming a part-time retirement business, such as an accountant, carpenter, salesperson or similar profession, you may be able to turn your experience into a small business after retirement.

Maybe you have a passion to do landscaping or own a small restaurant. You might consider a franchise opportunity in which you can eliminate some of the risks by following a turnkey system. We will explore the risks and benefits of both.

Unless you are financially prepared to expend funds to hire and train employees, you will most likely find yourself, again, **trading time for dollars**, but with additional financial exposure.

Instead of creating freedom, you will be further tied to the outcome of your work, and most likely experience reduced freedom because **now your own money is on the line**.

While there is additional risk in owning a small business, typically you do not create any leverage. **If you stop working, you stop earning.**

FRANCHISING – A TURNKEY SYSTEM

Franchises come in all sizes offering nearly every product or service imaginable.

Cost varies from a few thousand dollars to millions for the top franchises. The top 100 have significantly improved success rates, but there is still no guarantee you will succeed. If you want to own a top franchise, you will invest an average of $600,000 before you service your first customer.

Frankly, if you can afford a McDonald's franchise, you probably did not get past the second chapter of this book, so I am assuming that you do not have a couple extra million dollars lying around to invest.

A basic internet search yields 1,000's of packaged franchise businesses costing $25,000, or less. Many of the low cost opportunities are little more than a "business plan with a logo" and you are on your own.

One of my favorites is a Dog Poop Removal Service at the low fee of $38,500, which is described as a "turnkey package". You still have to market, hire employees (unless you plan to pick up the poop yourself), hire an accountant, attorney, obtain liability insurance, etc. You will invest time and money before you have one customer. How much poop will you have to scoop before you begin to turn a profit?

I hope you do not see me smiling as I write this, but it is plain to see you are typically buying a job with any small franchise. That is not all bad if you find something that fuels your passion.

What's the real issue with a traditional small business or small franchise? NO LEVERAGE! If you do not go to work, you do not get paid. How long will your health hold out? Do you want to be picking up poop in your 70's and 80's?

In the next chapter, we will explore the difference between a typical franchise and **"The People's Franchise"** which offers the best of what makes the franchise model attractive, without the large upfront fees and ongoing costs associated with owning and operating a small business.

The goal of many emerging small businesses is to become a "Big Business", but very few are able to make that transition.

3. BIG BUSINESS – OWN A SYSTEM

While this is certainly one of the most attractive options, it is generally not available to the average individual. The closest most people ever get to Big Business is investing their 401K or savings into stocks or mutual funds that own shares in these large enterprises.

By definition, *Big Business is large-scale, corporate-controlled, business activities. The term is typically used to describe activities that run from "huge transactions" to the more general "doing big things". Corporations that fall into the category of "Big Business" include Wal-Mart, Apple, Google, Microsoft, General Electric, General Motors, and Citigroup.*

While owning a Big Business may be highly desirable, and will certainly create leverage, we will not spend much time exploring this area since few of us will ever have that option.

4. INVESTOR

The fourth and final way to create income is to be an Investor. Many people participate on a limited basis in this category from within a 401k, stocks, annuities or other passive investments that generate income without shareholder participation.

If your passive investment income is sufficient to fund your lifestyle after retirement, you find yourself in an ideal situation. **However, if you must participate in the investment activity, it might actually be characterized as a small business, since it is not truly passive income.**

Network marketing companies are considered worthy financial investments, and many Big Businesses, including Citi-bank, Warren Buffet and Donald Trump have invested in network marketing company ownership.

Again, we will not spend much time on the Investor model as this option is available to only a few.

The traditional route works for many, but sometimes circumstances set your dreams in a different direction. Consider Jane's story.

DETOUR FROM THE TRADITIONAL ROUTE

Jane's parents raised her with this simple advice, "Get your degree. Get a job. Work hard." That is what she did. She earned her degree, began her career as a software programmer and worked hard to advance in her career.

She married, and had her first child, a son. Then, back to work.

When she became pregnant with her second child, a daughter, she was secretly trying to figure out how she could be a stay-at-home mom to her kids.

One day her nanny asked her why she wanted another child, when she did not have time for the one she already had. The realization hit her. She barely knew her own son.

A few months earlier, a friend had invited her to a meeting to learn about a business idea, and planted the thought in her mind that she could have her own business. She signed up that night to support her friend, but when the Distributor Kit came in the mail, she put the box on a shelf and never opened it. She stayed in touch with the friend, who was earning some money and excited about his future. He continued to encourage her to join him.

Then, the nanny asked her that question.

Now, where was that kit about that business?

Network marketing was foreign to everything she had known in the past, but she opened the box and began telling friends how she was going to "do this business" to stay home with her kids. Seven of them joined her in the first week.

Six months later, she was able to quit her corporate job and became a stay-at-home mom.

One thing certain about life is that it changes. Jane divorced and went back to what she knew was a safe-haven, software programming. Life stabilized, she remarried and moved to Arizona.

She soon remembered the freedom she had in her network marketing business and how she had been available to raise her kids. She wanted that freedom, again.

Commission checks, from the work she had done years earlier, were still coming in monthly, so when the thought of staying home became a passion, it was natural to turn to the company that she had represented in the past and pick up where she left off.

Get out that box, again.

Her first month back, she earned $660. The next month, $1900. By the end of the first year, her checks were averaging $2400 per month. At the end of the second year, they were averaging $3500 per month. That was more than she was earning as a software programmer with a college degree. But it was not simply the paycheck. It was the freedom to be home with her kids, participate in their activities and be there for them when they came home from school.

When Jane's father had a stroke, she was the only family member who had the freedom to pause her career and care for him for a period of two years. Throughout that time, her network marketing checks continued to arrive monthly, and she was averaging an income of over $4,000 per month for work that she had done years earlier.

Jane's kids are now college age and network marketing has taken on a second life as it often does.

At 52, Jane is now considering her retirement plan and understands how network marketing can create long-term residual income that will carry her through her retirement years.

Like any business, you will get out of it what you put into it. Network marketing is no different. There is no ceiling on your earning potential. Your results (and your paycheck) will be based on your own efforts.

Jane has begun working toward her goal of increasing her monthly check by $2,000. She says, "Why not? If you know how to earn $500 per month in network marketing, then you know how to earn $5,000 per month".

LET'S EXAMINE "THE PEOPLE'S FRANCHISE"

Hopefully, you have considered the four income options, eliminated the ones that are not available to you and opened your mind to an idea that millions of people believe is a better way, "The People's Franchise".

The richest people in the world look for and build Networks, everyone else looks for work

~Robert Kiyosaki, Author, *Rich Dad, Poor Dad*

CHAPTER 4

THE PEOPLE'S FRANCHISE

You can call it:

Social Marketing

Referral Marketing

Connection Marketing

Multi-level Marketing

Relationship Marketing

Direct Sales Marketing

For the purpose of clarity, we will use the term **"Network Marketing"** or **"NWM"** and call individual representatives in any company **"Distributors"**.

NETWORK MARKETING IS NOT AN "INDUSTRY".

It is a **DISTRIBUTION SYSTEM** designed to move products and services into the hands of consumers through the network of its distributors. It has proven to be enormously successful for over 60 years.

Manufacturers are looking to invest their advertising dollars as close to the point of sale as possible. That connection is exactly what network marketing offers. When you have coffee with a friend, and share a story of how a product or service worked for you and the benefits you received, it is the single most powerful method of reaching the end consumer.

It might be helpful to understand the **traditional business model**. Each time a product activity occurs in any phase of distribution, costs are incurred. It operates similar to this diagram.

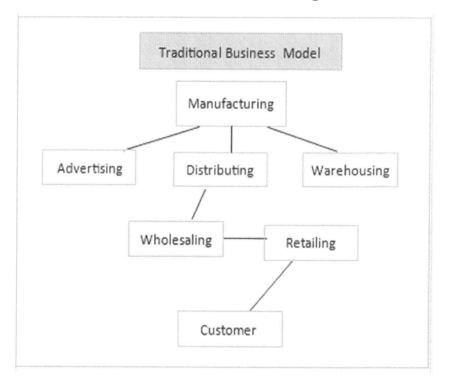

Network marketing uses a different model. The products move from the manufacturer directly to the end-consumer.

Most of the traditional distribution costs are eliminated, thus saving the company 20% to 40% of typical expenses.

The cost savings are passed to the network of distributors, in the form of compensation, for introducing the customer to the company. It is a simple, but brilliant concept.

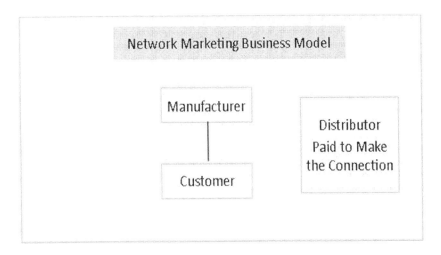

Network Marketing is neither good nor bad. It is a distribution method for products and services, and it boasts some pretty impressive numbers.

15.9 million people in the U.S. are involved

$28.5 billion in total U.S. sales in 2011

$117 billion in sales worldwide

Some people QUIT, other make MILLIONS in the same company. The opportunity is equal for both. I hope to help you understand the reasons behind success and failure, and provide information that will increase the likelihood that you will achieve your goals.

WHAT MOTIVATES YOU?

While the motivation is slightly different for each person, **most distributors fall into at least one of six categories**. However, as success is achieved in one category, many distributors move to another category.

1. **Discount buyers** – These distributors are mainly interested in buying products they use and love at a discount. They place regular orders for their own use and do not actively sell or recruit others. In 2011, it was estimated that **29%** of all participants join for this purpose. It is one of the reasons why NWM's unique, high-quality products are found in **three out of every four households** in America.

2. **Goal seekers** – These distributors have a specific, short-term plan. Goal seekers may desire to earn extra money for a family vacation or a special project. In many cases, goal seekers will drop out after having achieved their goal and then re-join when they have another short-term goal in mind.

3. **Part-timers** – These individuals are looking for supplemental income, and are very likely to continue in the business for an extended period. They are looking for a steady flow of extra income, often a modest amount such as $200 to $500 per month. They will likely spend less than five to ten hours per week on their business. **36%** of all network marketers identify themselves in this category.

4. **Recognition and Rewards** – Distributors in this group love to receive recognition and rewards for their achievements and find this element of network marketing to be extremely appealing. It would be difficult to find a traditional workplace that recognizes and rewards achievement as regularly or as publicly as network marketing.

5. **Product advocates** – Like discount buyers, this group of distributors use and love the products or services. However, they also want to share that passion with others. Promoting the product or service is very fulfilling to them because they believe in the benefits of what they are representing so strongly that they want to share them with others who might find similar benefit. According to the Direct Sellers Association, **57% of all full-time network marketers began as discount buyers or product advocates.**

6. **Entrepreneurs** – This group is looking for full-time income. These distributors will dedicate 30+ hours per week to building their business and will often be active recruiters. They generally enjoy the opportunity to train and motivate others and consider their network marketing activities as their profession.

Once you understand the variety of reasons people join network marketing, it is easier to understand why there is such a variance in incomes. A $500 monthly income would mean success if that was the person's original goal. **Network marketing provided them with exactly what they set out to accomplish**.

It is the primary reason that **83% of all network marketers rate their experience as "very good" or "excellent".** That satisfaction number is close to the top rating of any job or profession.

The average age of a network marketer today is 44 years old.

40% of all current network marketers have been with the same company **more than five years**.

Once you begin to understand the potential of network marketing, you might ask yourself the same question I did.

"So why isn't everyone doing this?"

A good question!

When you think about network marketing, what comes to mind? Did you try it yourself and not succeed? Did a friend become an overly zealous product-pusher and turn you off to the concept? Were you invited to the home of a friend only to find a white-board in the dining room instead of dinner? While that would never be condoned by any network marketing professional, these stories have circulated until many believe them to be standard practice, which is far from the truth. Your own experience, or stories heard from others, whether true or not, will affect your thinking.

If we encounter a pushy car salesperson, we still purchase cars. We simply find another salesperson that will treat us with respect. When you have a rude clerk at a store, you don't stop buying groceries. You go to a different checkout line next time.

This book is intended to present the facts of this profession and the benefits it can offer the average person, which are not available in any other small business. The goal is education and understanding. Are you open to consider changes in your thinking?

ANTI-RECESSION BUSINESS

NWM companies have enjoyed consistent, steady growth year after year, and have experienced surprising spikes during each of the past six recessions (see figure below). When the job supply is lower than the demand, people often seek part-time income to fill in the "earnings gap".

GROWTH OF NWM IN PAST RECESSIONS

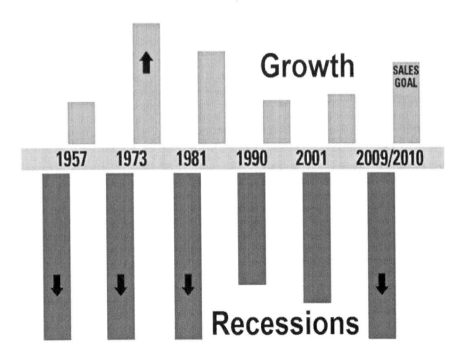

Network marketing provides the opportunity to create additional income while continuing to work a primary job. The majority of network marketers begin their career on-the-side of their current occupation.

Network marketing offers a creditable way for anyone to own their own business, earn a substantial income, and contribute to others. It offers comparatively low risk and affordable start-up costs. The profession is open to any race, sex, education, religion, social standing, family background, business experience or education, regardless of past success or failure.

The **only common predictor of success** is a burning desire to achieve a goal and a willingness to work for a better life or a higher purpose.

An interesting statistic from the Direct Sellers Association reflects that **an increasing number of men** are participating in the profession.

In 2007, 14% of network marketers were male. Four years later, that number had increased to 22%. Top male earners are in every company, including skin care and household products.

I was personally concerned that the cost to start a network marketing business was so low that it just couldn't work, and I certainly could not make "big money". But, I did my research and asked the right questions, of the right people. I soon became convinced that if I developed the needed skills and followed a plan for three to five years, I could build a successful business. The only limits would be those I placed on myself.

As we go through this information, I suggest you keep a list of any unanswered questions. Hopefully we will cover them along the way.

We briefly discussed the concept of LEVERAGE in describing the four ways to earn an income. We saw that income from personal employment is limited by the amount of hours a person has available in any day, week or month.

The secret to network marketing's continued success is based on **two concepts of LEVERAGE**.

DIRECT COMPENSATION

In network marketing, you are paid commissions and bonuses monthly, on your own purchases, and purchases made by your customers and their referrals. As your active customer count grows, so does your paycheck. There are no limits to the rewards you can earn. Build a small personal network, earn small rewards. Build a big personal network, earn big rewards.

INDIRECT COMPENSATION

As a leader, you will teach, coach and motivate the distributors on your team. As they become more effective at the skills of building a network, **their team grows, and your team grows.** You can expand you network throughout the state, the country, and if your company offers international opportunities, you can build a global profit center.

Once the network is established and operating on its own for the most part, you have created time and financial freedom in your own life.

THE HOLY GRAIL - RESIDUAL INCOME

This is the ability to be paid, over and over again, for work that you do one time.

There are a few industries that provide residual income. Musicians, authors, and insurance sales are some examples. If you were to write or record a popular song, each time that song was played on the radio, or a CD was sold, you could receive a royalty payment.

Residual income is considered highly desirable retirement income because it allows you to put in effort once, and reap the rewards for months and years to come.

This is one reason why "consumable" products are the most effective in network marketing. Consumable products are bought, used, and then replaced, over and over again.

FRANCHISING VS. NETWORK MARKETING

A traditional franchise is a form of a network, made up of business owners, working together under a licensed company umbrella for their own individual benefit. If you want to create additional profit centers (locations), you will pay additional franchise fees, overhead, etc.

Network marketing consists of a network of "authorized" (franchised) distributors. As a business form, it is often called "The People's Franchise."

In addition to low cost and ease of entry, network marketers have the right to expand their market reach and open additional profit centers by enlarging their network.

You don't pay to add additional profit centers, but instead are paid on the result your new network produces.

While both are considered small business activities, let's take a head-to-head look at the differences between a typical franchise and a network marketing business.

TYPICAL FRANCHISE	NETWORK MARKETING
$25,000 to $1.8 Million	Less than $1,000
Brick and Mortar (rent)	Work From Home
Employees	No Employees
Fixed Location	Global Potential
Inventory	No Inventory
HIGH Risk	LOW Risk
Long Fixed Hours	Set Your Hours
Limited Freedom	Time Freedom

In a typical franchise, you are responsible for bookkeeping, banking and all customer service.

In network marketing, the company keeps track of your customers, distributors and their activities, which you can generally view in "real-time" on a company provided business management website.

The company will provide you with an IRS form 1099 at the end of each year stating your total income. You will file and pay your own taxes, just as any business owner would do.

Most companies offer top-of–the-line websites for a very nominal monthly fee. This is a tremendous time and financial load off the distributor.

The company is typically responsible for all product delivery and support. You won't have to move the car out of the garage or give up your closet space. Stocking inventory, in most network marketing companies, is a thing of the past.

In a typical network marketing company, you will be compensated for three activities. It is important to focus your efforts in these three areas.

1. Your OWN production

2. The production of others that YOU bring into the network

3. The production of others that THEY bring into the network

GOOD OR BAD,

YOU WILL BE PAID ON WHAT YOU PRODUCE!

You job is not sales. **Your primary job is to teach, train and motivate your team**.

Your team may grow slowly in the beginning, so you will need to stick with your plan. You could build a serious income at lunch, 15 minute breaks, before and after work coffee meetings, evenings and weekends.

You will likely sponsor many people during your career, but your big income growth will typically come from two to five people.

To find the two to five, you will most likely sponsor 20 to 50 distributors interested in building a business during the course of your career. How fast you do that is up to you.

Some will build, some won't. Some will do less than they promise, others will see the potential and do more. Some will revert to customers, while some customers will decide to build. Your job is to help them succeed, where they are currently, and encourage their individual goals.

OFFLINE OR ONLINE

There is constant debate about the right or wrong way to build a network. As someone who began by building a local network, and subsequently built an internet based network, I have been on both sides, and they both work.

It simply has to do with your personal interests and circumstances. **The skills of a network marketing professional, which we will discuss further in Chapter 11, translate to both offline and online marketing.**

However you generate your network, it is important to understand that people prefer to do business with someone they KNOW, LIKE and TRUST.

While you can make one-time product sales both online or offline. Customers, regardless of the source, will generally not make further purchases without follow up.

Rarer still, will someone join you as a business building distributor without a personal connection, regardless of how brief.

If you love the face-to-face interaction, that's the way you should build. I love meeting people one to one and sharing my experience with the products and the business.

I also love working in my PJ's, sipping coffee in my comfortable home office, so I combine them. Each can be successful and fulfilling if you follow a process, and continue to interact with your customers and distributors on a regular basis.

It would be difficult to succeed in any business today without basic computer tools such as e-mail and internet access, so be prepared to learn a few new things if you don't already have that knowledge.

While Social Media is not required, I encourage all distributors to create a Facebook or Google + profile. These are the largest "phonebooks" in the world and the best way for you to find and connect with people. If you respect the rules of "net-iquette", you will have fun re-connecting with old friends and making new ones.

I love stories. It is what this profession is all about. My favorites are those unlikely heroes of the business. As you read, consider the background of the individual and say to yourself, "If she can do it, I can do it". That is Lorraine's goal in sharing her story with you.

THE NETWORK MARKETING LIFESTYLE

At the age of 43, Lorraine had four teenage daughters approaching college age and needed some additional income. She had a full-time job, but her income was not going to meet the increasing need of the next several years. The girls were beginning to communicate with colleges and Lorraine and her husband, Carl wanted to make the finances work.

They looked at a variety of franchise opportunities, but just couldn't swing the large up-front fee to get started.

One day, a patient in the medical office where Lorraine worked left a business card and a small product sample on her desk. Eventually, Lorraine met with the woman's sponsor at a local coffee shop, listened to a presentation, and immediately recognized that this could be the solution she had been seeking.

The woman's sponsor told her she would have to learn a few new skills, including how to teach, coach and mentor others. Her immediate response was, "I can do that. In fact, it sounds like fun".

Lorraine began her new business on a part-time basis. Within ten months, her part-time income equaled the income she was earning working full time. She quit her job and never looked back.

The business soon created enough income that her husband was able to retire earlier than originally scheduled. They supported each other in further building the business, and their life together was full and rewarding.

Five years later, the girls were all off to college preparing for their future careers.

One day, Carl did not return home at the expected time, which was unlike him. Shortly thereafter, two police cars pulled up in front of the house. Two uniformed officers got out of the vehicles and started up the driveway. Lorraine knew immediately that her husband would not be coming home.

He was found in his car in the Walgreen's parking lot at the end of their street, dead from a heart attack.

Lorraine is very grateful for the five years they shared together, working their network marketing business and getting to know each other again before he passed away.

Carl had a small retirement income of $880 per month, which was cut to $440 at the time of his death. Within three years, his insurance benefits were cancelled.

Thanks to her network marketing business, Lorraine was able to maintain the lifestyle she and Carl had created for their family.

Today at 80 years old, Lorraine has re-married and lives in comfort. She has enjoyed a 6-figure income for the past 18 years and has wonderful memories of the trips she has taken, the cars she has earned and the rewards of working with a great network of fun-loving, caring people.

Lorraine is not done yet. There are people she wants to help, and causes to which she wants to contribute. She loves every day that she makes a difference in someone's life. She is setting goals for that next trip and achievement. Go Lorraine!

SO MANY REASONS

Money is a great motivator. Let's discuss some additional reasons why you might want to have a business of your own.

A lot of people are afraid to say what they want, that's why they don't get what they want.

~ Madonna

CHAPTER 5

A BUSINESS OF YOUR OWN

Remember when you were young, and someone would ask you, "What are you going to be when you grow up?" You mind was filled with possibilities. There was nothing you could not do, be, or accomplish. You believed you could be an astronaut, a movie star, an Olympic swimmer or even the president. What happened to those dreams?

We live in a world of well-intentioned people who think they are helping to prepare us for life's disappointments, with statements like, "Don't get your hopes up" or, "That idea won't work". In the process, they can unintentionally dampen our enthusiasm for what we can accomplish. If you hear it enough, you start to believe it, even when there is evidence to the contrary.

Yet, **70% of all adults continue to express the desire to own their own business.** Here are the TOP TEN reasons people give for wanting to own a business:

Be their own boss

Time freedom / own their own life

Financial freedom

Retirement or residual income

Desire to work from home

Be more available to family or friends

Leave a legacy

Recognition for their achievements

Support people or causes they believe in

Tax advantages

Owning a small business can provide some of the desired goals above, but **only** network marketing claims it can provide them all.

When my first company in network marketing went bankrupt after eight years, I did not consider a traditional business although I had the drive and confidence to succeed. I was unwilling to give up the benefits that only network marketing had provided.

You have to choose whom you will listen to. Those who say you can't or those who believe you can. Often, people who try to kill the dreams of others have given up on their own dreams.

Top motivational speakers say that your life will be the average of the five people with whom you spend the most time. Is it time to add a few new friends into your life that have dreams and are reaching for them?

Fortunately, I had an entrepreneurial father who believed I could do anything I truly wanted. He encouraged my dreams. So, when well-meaning friends told me it was not possible, I chose to believe my dad. That belief has served me well.

TOP REASONS FOR <u>NOT</u> STARTING A BUSINESS

Starting your own business may seem like an ideal way to achieve the goals of freedom and money. Yet **less than 10%** actually ever attempt it. What stops them? Here are the top four reasons given:

- Time commitment
- Financial Investment
- Fear
- Unsupportive partner or family

Starting a **traditional small business** will typically require your full time, attention and a significant financial investment. There is often a genuine fear of expending time and money and not succeeding. In a traditional business, you will often lose money for the first one to three years.

If you decide on **network marketing**, two of the primary benefits are the small investment and the ability to begin on a part-time basis.

Many distributors actually earn a profit in their first month. You'll have the support of the company and your sponsor. Together, they will eliminate most of the fear and guesswork that often comes with striking out on your own.

The obstacle that you might encounter in both scenarios is unsupportive family or friends. They may not understand why you would leave the security or prestige of a job for the **potential** rewards of business ownership. For the true entrepreneur, the answer is obvious, they are seeking the time and financial freedom that a business of their own can offer.

When you look at owners of traditional small businesses, you often see a high-energy entrepreneur with excellent skills and the drive to succeed.

The most impressive thing about network marketing is the variety of individuals who achieve success. Housewives to doctors, coaches to corporate executives, sales and non-sales backgrounds alike. Grade school education, high school education, advanced degrees; we all have a level playing field. It's up to you to determine the result. **It is not about where you start, it's about where you finish.**

Activity matters most. Examine your core values and see if you have what it takes to move from a traditional mindset to an owner's mindset.

YOUR CORE VALUES

Ask yourself these questions

- Do I truly want to change my future?

- Do I like helping people?

- Do I enjoy learning and teaching new ideas and concepts?

- Am I willing to invest two to three years to learn the skills of a professional network marketer?

For the most part, **education trains people to be employees, not business owners.** You are going to have to think differently.

Small Dreams, Small Life! Big Dreams, Big Life!

LEARNING CURVE

You don't know what you don't know!

Figure out what you don't know and learn it!

Like any business, the secret to success, isn't really a secret. It's dedication, persistence and constantly improving your skills.

Most people fail because they quit too soon. Success does not by-pass the team, it will just by-pass them.

If you had invested $400,000 in a Franchise business, and the first few weeks or months were slower than anticipated, would you just give back the keys, lock the door and quit. Of course not! But, because network marketing has a low entry fee, people are often quick to quit when success doesn't come as soon as they had hoped, or when someone they care about says no to their idea.

RECOGNITION AND ACHIEVEMENT

The thrill of being applauded by your peers and recognized by corporate founders and executives is often a career high that happens rarely if ever, in traditional business or employment.

In network marketing, you don't have to wait for the proverbial gold watch or 20-year pin. You will take a bow and earn applause from your very first achievements. Peer recognition earns applause from family and friends, as well.

Recognition for achievements, both great and small, are key components of network marketing.

In addition, opportunities abound to earn incentive trips and dream vacations. Whether it's a cruise to Hawaii, a trip to Europe, or a weekend in the wine country, these earned incentives are often trips that most people only dream of experiencing. Other incentives range from jewelry to automobiles. Rewarding and celebrating success fuels the network marketing profession.

WRITE YOUR OWN STORY

When all is said and done, network marketing is an opportunity to write your own story. It's about setting goals and achieving them. It's about building a business that is uniquely you. It's about your family, no one else's. It's about your dream. It's about your family's dream. It's about falling in love with your own life. Go ahead, do something for yourself that you'll love.

YOU MIGHT EVEN LIVE LONGER

I actually enjoyed my real estate business and the success and recognition it brought. But the personal cost was too high. The stress associated with employees, constant legal issues, 80-hour work weeks, and no time for myself, eventually took its toll. My decision to walk away and become a full time network marketer literally saved my life. Most people don't get boxed into such a dramatic corner, but the constant stress of a job or traditional business will eventually be felt in your life and health.

Leisure-time physical activity is associated with longer life expectancy, according to a study by researchers led by the National Cancer Institute (NCI). The study found that people who engaged in leisure-time physical activity had **life expectancy gains of as much as 4.5 years**.

Speaking of leisure reminds me of my friend Rod, who loves nothing more than standing on the riverbank in his waders, catching and releasing world-class trout from his own back yard.

A SIMPLE INVITATION

Rod began his career in network marketing at the age of 21, after responding to a single question from his boss in the record sales business. "Could you use an extra $1,000 per month?" Rod said, "Sure".

As a young married man with an 18-month old daughter, he was looking for ways to supplement his income. The timing was perfect. Rod met with his boss at a coffee shop, and in about 20 minutes using a simple brochure, his boss explained the basic concept of the business and how money was earned.

Rod said that he "knew that he knew", even at 21 years old, that network marketing would be his financial future and his retirement program.

Rod followed the plan that his boss laid out for him. Within eight months, he was making more money part-time, then he was making at his full-time job. He quit his day job and became a full-time network marketer.

As Rod's income grew, so did his family, which eventually included five children. Rod was able to be a stay-at-home dad and attend school plays in the morning, sporting events in the afternoon and concerts in the evening. Often he was the only dad in attendance. He was able to work his business around the family schedule, rather than having to fit his family life into his work schedule.

Network marketing became a family affair when Rod's dad, who had been a career church pastor, retired without sufficient income to live a comfortable life. Rod introduced him to the business idea, and he began his career in network marketing at the age of 65. For the next 6 years, he averaged $2,100 per month in income, earned three bonus cars and helped many people, which was his true passion.

The Second Round

34 years later, Rod's kids have grown and are establishing families of their own. He is an avid sportsman, and he and his wife, Danette love the outdoors. They dreamed of moving to a remote location in northern Michigan to enjoy their retirement years.

Two years ago, they realized that dream when they moved into their new home, located on 22 acres, with frontage on a blue ribbon trout stream, in the Huron National Forest.

A network marketing business is portable and basically requires a computer, a phone and an internet connection. So, from their dream home on the river, Rod continues to support his team and add to his already 6-figure retirement income.

What a fabulous account of a life-well-lived and dreams that came true. Just for inspiration, I have included another story that is one of my favorites. I know of no better way for everyday people to create a family legacy than through network marketing.

A FIVE-GENERATION LEGACY

Kindness to a stranger who was left standing on the sidewalk when his appointment for the afternoon was not at home, led to a legacy network marketing business that spans five generations.

Robin's Grandmother, Helen, was looking out her front window and saw a frustrated gentleman waiting outside her next-door neighbor's home. The neighbor had left without cancelling their scheduled appointment. Grandma Helen opened the door and asked the fellow if he would like a glass of water.

He explained that he was there to talk to the neighbor about a business that she could run from home. Grandma Helen kindly invited him in and offered to listen to the presentation.

She purchased some products and six months later, after sharing them with family and friends, she was driving the first of many bonus cars and earning a steady income from her new business.

Eventually, she introduced the idea to her son, Bob and his wife, Emily. Initially, they were not interested as her son had a successful insurance business. But when Grandma Helen showed him her IRS 1099 form, he discovered that she was earning more in her part time business than he earned working full time as an insurance broker. That made the decision a little easier.

Bob, Emily, and their daughter Robin worked together in the business for 17 years. Spending time with family you enjoy is a wonderful benefit of owning a successful family-operated business.

Today, Robin and her husband Carl lead the third generation of their network marketing business.

Following in the family tradition, Robin's oldest daughter has earned a company leadership position, in her own right, and is looking forward to joining the partnership as a fourth generation business owner. Robin's granddaughter, who is 17, is already excited about joining them as soon as she turns 18.

Their business generates an average of $500,000 per year in commissions and a lifestyle that many only dream of living. They have enjoyed fabulous international trips as a family, drive company provided cars and most importantly, have affected the lives of 10,000's of others throughout their network.

The business has provided a source of funding to help many of their extended family, as well. For Robin and Carl, it is not only about the money, but the many family and friends that they have been able to touch through the products and business benefits they have been able to share with others. What a legacy.

WHAT <u>ARE</u> YOU LOOKING FORWARD TO?

Another day of waking up to the alarm clock?

Another day of leaving your kids at day care?

Another day of going to work for someone else?

Another day not spent with your family?

Another day spent in fear of your future?

Another year without a vacation?

Another year gone by, and your retirement still has a BIG gap?

WHAT <u>COULD</u> YOU LOOK FORWARD TO?

Waking up with a new outlook on life!

Be there to see your kids and grand-kids grow up!

Going to work for yourself!

Having time to spend with your family!

The time and money to take a vacation!

Making real plans for the future!

A secure retirement plan

Don't make assumptions! Find the courage to ask questions and to express what you really want. Communicate with others as clearly as you can to avoid misunderstandings, sadness and drama.

~ Miguel Angel Ruiz

CHAPTER 6

ANSWERS TO THE TOP TEN QUESTIONS OR CONCERNS

Every network marketer should welcome questions from potential customers or distributors. Consider each question an opportunity to educate and bring understanding of the profession, whether the person decides to join you or not.

As you respond to questions, you will generally discover that they stem from one of two areas of concern:

Lack of confidence in their own abilities

Lack of understanding of network marketing

We will address the Top Ten most asked questions or stated concerns. If your specific question is not included, ask your potential sponsor. If they don't know the answer, they will find it for you.

Don't allow an unanswered question to stop you from pursuing your dreams.

1. I DON'T HAVE TIME

It really is a question of priorities.

What if we took a look at your schedule and found that you have an uncommitted 5 to 10 hours in your week?

Since we all have the same 168 hours available each week. Let's make some "average" calculations:

Activity	Average	YOU
Sleep (7 hours each night)	49	_____
Job (includes travel time)	50	_____
Meals (3 hours/day)	21	_____
Family/Friends (2 hours/day)	14	_____
Miscellaneous (2 hours/day)	<u>14</u>	_____
Total Hours Per Week	148	_____

Surprise! Most people have 20 unallocated hours EVERY WEEK. Now, **Calculate your own number**.

Where does the time go? Nielsen Statistics report that **the average person spends 34 hours per week watching TV and another 5 hours surfing the internet**. Imagine what you could accomplish using those same hours building your future.

If you were willing to invest time now, you could join the ranks of TV watchers later. Or, you may find your new profession so fulfilling, both personally and financially, you won't want to waste those long hours watching someone else live life. You'll be living life on your own terms.

2. I DON'T WANT TO BUG MY FRIENDS

Here's the thing! YOU DON"T HAVE to ask any of them to buy your products or look at your business if you don't want. But here's A TRUTH. You DO need to tell them what you are doing and ask for their support. Let me explain.

Let's step out of network marketing for a minute. Let's say you opened an athletic shoe store in your town. Would you keep your new business a secret from your family and friends? Of course not! Would you invite total strangers to your Grand Opening or would you invite your family and friends?

If your friends don't wear athletic shoes for some reason, will you get mad if they don't make a purchase? Of course not! But you would ask them to refer their friends who do use similar products, right?

Maybe one day they will decide to get in shape and begin walking two miles every day. Since you told them about your products, it would only be natural for them to come to you when the time is right. If you didn't tell them, that would be your mistake.

There is a difference between being proud of what you do and forcing people to buy from you. Any pushy salesperson in any industry can cause a negative reaction among friends. But an approach as simple as, "Bill, I don't expect you to make a purchase from me, unless you see something you like. But, I would like to share my product line with you in case you, or someone you know, may have a need in the future."

When sharing the business, you might say, "Mary, I know you were looking for some extra income to pay for private school for the kids. I don't know if what I'm doing would be a good fit for you, but I would like to ask for 30 minutes of your time. If you're not interested, that's okay, but you might know someone you could refer to me".

It's all about learning the skills of connecting with people, telling your story and asking them to "take a look".

I'll be honest, it stings a bit when a family member or friend says no, but frankly if you are proud of what you are doing and persevere, some will join you later if you respect their decision today. They may just want to see if you will "stick with it".

Remember, one important fact. You may know a few hundred or maybe even a few thousand people. But, there are literally **billions of people you don't know** and have never met. One of the skills you will learn is how and where to meet new people who might have an interest in your products or business.

3. I DON'T HAVE THE MONEY TO BEGIN

This can be a challenging issue, particularly when it comes from someone, seemingly successful, who catches you off guard by admitting they don't have $300 (or whatever the cost) to join you.

Respectfully, my first question is always: "Sam, IF you had the $300, would you make the decision to join me?" This will help uncover whether it is simply an excuse, or there is a real issue.

If they really don't have the money, you need to realize that they NEED your business more than they may be willing to admit. I am no longer shocked when a college professor, a corporate executive or a career banker tells me they don't have the money to join.

The next step is to ask, "Sam, if we spent a few minutes finding a source of $300, would that help your decision?"

Then, brainstorm some examples of where they could generate the money. Over the years I have worked with a variety of individuals who did some difficult things in order to create a long-term plan for themselves and their families including:

> Held a Garage Sale
> Sold an X-Box
> Borrowed from a family member
> Took a credit card advance
> Sold their big screen TV

If people are not willing to sacrifice for a better future, they probably are not truly interested. Let them go. In 17 years, I have never met a person who sincerely wanted to join that did not find the money.

One other option exists in most companies. It can have a variety of names, but let's call it a "starter kit". It includes basic business building information for a smaller fee, usually between $20 - $99. While I rarely recommend this option, because it usually does not include needed tools or any products, it is something to consider when there is simply no other way, and they truly want to join you.

4. ARE THE PRODUCTS MORE EXPENSIVE?

Sometimes, the answer is, "yes" if there is a discernible quality difference. But, **just as often, the products are equally priced or less expensive** because of a savings in distribution costs.

Products sold through network marketing often have a unique story that requires a personal demonstration or additional information. Some products are exclusive to network marketing. Items we consider commonplace today, such as vacuum cleaners, sewing machines and green household cleaners were initially introduced to the public through the network marketing concept. Each required an explanation or a demonstration. That is the role of the distributor.

As you start to consider a network marketing company, I encourage you to find their **Unique Selling Proposition** (USP). Listen to the main points with an open mind. If you are not convinced, it is unlikely that you will be successful in taking that product to your network.

For example, 23% of network marketing companies produce a nutrition line. Since you can walk into any major store and see a wall of nutrition products, find out what makes the company's product unique. It will probably convince you of the need for the information to be delivered by a network of informed distributors. Often, a USP requires a comparison or information that the public is not generally aware of, but once convinced, will become a devotee of those same products, even if the price were the same, or slightly higher.

5. I'M NOT A SALESPERSON

Speaking as someone who spent nearly 30 years in sales, I can definitely say that sales experience can actually be a hindrance to success.

To build a successful network marketing team, you need to be able to train 100's or 1,000's to do what you do in a duplicable manner. Since less than 5% of the population consider themselves "sales types", trained sales people have an instant problem.

Successful network marketing professionals understand that if they have a clear system, teach the necessary skills, and keep sales-ability out of the equation, anyone will be able to follow the process.

Tools that **do the work** of explaining the products and business opportunity best accomplish this. Most successful companies produce simple tools such as DVD's or Websites that do the "selling" for you. This is one of the recommendations we will explore further in the next several chapters.

6. WHAT WOULD I BE DOING?

In Network Marketing, you will do 3 things:

 a. Use the products
 b. Share the products and business idea
 c. Teach new distributors to do **a**. and **b.**

Improving your skills will improve your success, but there is no substitute for enthusiasm. Be excited about the new products you are experiencing. Learn to ask for interest in both the products and the business. Tell the whole story.

If the conversation begins with products, because that is the original interest, always have a follow up conversation to provide information about the business. If they are not interested, thank them, then ask for a referral to someone who might have an interest.

Studying your products and learning more about your new profession are worthwhile activities. However, you should **spend 80% of your allocated time** presenting and training the products, the business, or both.

IF YOU WILL **GET OUT OF THE LIBRARY**, YOU CAN **GO TO THE BANK**. Yes, you will make mistakes, but you will quickly learn from them and constantly improve your skills.

7. KNOW PEOPLE OR A COMPANY THAT FAILED

Whether a traditional business or a network marketing company, the failure rate is about 80% of EVERY NEW BUSINESS. It is one of the reasons we suggest that you do the research recommended in this book, before making a decision to join any company.

Ex-employees of closed or bankrupt traditional businesses usually see themselves as **victims of a bad economy**; whereas, ex-distributors of closed network marketing companies often consider themselves **victims of the company** or the network marketing concept.

If a restaurant owner, real estate salesperson or a car mechanic fails, they typically blame the economy.

If a network marketing distributor fails, they will often say that it wasn't a good product, company or pay plan, yet many **members in that same company are creating wealth and rewards**.

The secret to success is to decide on products you believe in, a compensation plan that fits your goals, a solid company with experience in network marketing and a sponsor that will help you learn the skills of success. The rest is up to you. Network marketing is simple, but it is not always easy. You have to actually DO IT!

Better yet, let's talk about why people succeed.

They treat their business like a real business and not a hobby. If you do, it will pay you like a real business. You will need to set goals like any business owner, then put a plan in place to reach them. Your sponsor will help you to set achievable goals based on your individual circumstances.

Success is not always visible immediately. Stay the course. Don't even think about quitting. If you do, re-hire yourself immediately.

Don't try to "re-invent the wheel". Your team leaders will teach you a plan that has created the success you desire, using a process they know will work.

Understand that many people join network marketing to earn an extra $500 - $1000 per month. Millions have achieved that goal. Every one of them is a success! Don't compare your idea of success to others. Instead, embrace the goals you have set and recognize others when they achieve their personal goals.

8. IS NETWORK MARKETING LEGAL?

I am always surprised when I get asked this question. Network marketing is a **60+ year old product distribution method**. Yet, some well-meaning people confuse it with illegal activity, called a "pyramid". Pyramids are illegal, plain and simple.

In the 1960's, **Congress came within 11 votes of declaring the Franchise Model an "Illegal Pyramid". In 2011, franchising accounted for over $800 billion in global sales.** We sometimes (even Congress) fear what we don't understand.

Like every business, the Federal Trade Commission, the Securities and Exchange Commission, the US Postal Service, the Internal Revenue Service, and most states Attorneys General also monitor business activities. A company that has been in business for five years, or more, generally has a track record with these agencies and you should feel comfortable that it is operating within the law.

9. I HAVE NO EXPERIENCE.

Network marketing is simple, but you can complicate it. If you follow the process set out by the company and your team, you can succeed.

Begin working right away on improving or developing the seven skills you will need throughout your career. We discuss them briefly in Chapter 11, then recommend a resource book that will go into greater depth on each skill. The good news is that they are all learn-able. You will find that developing these skills will benefit you in your everyday life, as well.

10. I DON'T HAVE A BIG NETWORK

Many people have this thought until they look at their social media page, cell phone contacts, and their e-mail list.

Think about where you shop and play, where you work and have worked, organizations you participate in and your local church. Think about all the small businesses that you frequent every week and those that provide services to you regularly.

Your sponsor will help you develop the list further, but it is said that anyone who has reached the age of 30 knows 2,000 people by name and those same people will know them by name. Remember, that's just the people YOU know!

What about the people THEY know and can refer to you? If you ask with the right attitude, people will often give you one or more names that were not on your original list. Be referable!

And, what about the people you meet, on purpose or as you are living your life.

Not enough for you yet?
There are networking organizations in most cities such as:

> Business Networkers International
> Meetup.com
> LeTip
> Heartlink

Do an internet search on "networking groups" in your area.

You get the idea. As long as you are willing to put yourself in a situation where you can meet new people and make new friends, you will never run out of prospects.

There are few people in the world who understand this profession better than my friend John who is a well-known author, yet has decided to return to his roots in network marketing.

NETWORKER – AUTHOR – NETWORKER

An icon to network marketers around the world, John Fogg is the best-selling author of numerous books and audios about the profession. He is best known for writing the industry classic, *The Greatest Networker in the World*, which has sold more than one million copies.

John began his career in network marketing as a distributor with some success. But he saw a need in the profession for teaching and training and felt that was his calling.

For over 25 years, John has been a much sought after speaker on the international stage and has positively influenced the lives of anyone who has been the beneficiary of his work.

The publishing industry has changed dramatically over the last 10 years. John decided to return to the profession he knew he was best suited for, and would support his financial goals, network marketing.

"I'm unemployable", John states. "Who would hire a 65 year old independent, creative thinker, who has been self-employed for 30 years, *and* insists on being a stay-at-home dad to his two young daughters (Ele is eleven and Anais is seven years old)? Besides, when you look around, what else is there?"

Today, John is a successful network marketer himself, working from his home using the internet to build a team surrounded by the people he loves.

Talking to John on the phone, you often hear the sounds of a violin, harp or piano in the background as he unapologetically shares his love of music with his children.

John's simple formula for business-building success, learned years ago, is still the foundation for building a team of independent entrepreneurs in today's digital age.

Connect > Engage > Enroll

John says, "Network Marketing has been, is, and always will be relationship-based. Inter-Network Marketing on Social Media such as Facebook is the perfect marriage of high-tech and high-touch." Which is why, he believes, "There has never been a better time for network marketing".

DID YOU GET YOUR QUESTIONS ANSWERED?

I hope you see that there are **real answers** to your questions and that network marketing is not only a legitimate way to achieve your income goals, but that it is a preferable way, particularly when it comes to building passive retirement income.

In the next four chapters, we will look at how to:

Select PRODUCTS that are a fit for you

Find a PAY PLAN that meets your goals

Research a CORPORATE PARTNER

Interview potential SPONSORS

Following this process will give you the confidence that you have the information you need should you decide to join this 60+ year profession that is meeting and exceeding the goals of millions.

No matter what your product is, you are ultimately in the education business. Your customers need to be constantly educated about the many advantages of doing business with you, trained to use your products more effectively, and taught how to make never-ending improvements in their lives.

~ Robert G. Allen

CHAPTER 7

YOU GOTTA BELIEVE IN THE PRODUCTS

Once you understand what you are looking for, it will take much of the stress out of your search. In fact, the process can actually be fun.

It is like dating in search of the right partner. It is not that there's anything wrong with any other product, you are simply looking to find the right fit for you.

In spite of comments to the contrary, there is NO PERFECT COMPANY. If you ask every network marketer, THEIR products are "the BEST on the market". Nothing compares. **That is exactly how they should feel.** Enthusiasm is a key ingredient to success. You may have to sift through a lot of "the BEST" to find products that are right for you.

Believe it or not, you may already be using them in your home.

I was a product customer of my current company for many years. No one told me there was an income opportunity available, so I did not have the option to consider the business until many years later.

By the time my initial network marketing company filed bankruptcy, I had become aware of that fact, and the company was placed into consideration. Our team still completed the search process, but when it came to deciding on products we felt we could believe in, I shared a strong product testimonial. Because the company met our other criteria, the team agreed that it was a good choice for our new home.

Take a look at a few of the product categories offered. In most cases, there are multiple companies in each category, and many companies cover more than one category.

PRODUCTS	**SERVICES**
Weight Loss	Legal Services
Nutrition	Communications
Housewares	Utilities
Cleaning Products	Greeting Cards
Skin care/Cosmetics	Medical/Dental
Clothing	Travel Services
Sports Drinks	Insurance
Essential Oils	Computer Services

I could add to the list, but I think you get the idea. Nearly every consumable/renewable product or service can be marketed through the network marketing distribution model.

Each time I use the term "products", I am referring to the products available from service companies, as well.

The key is to select products you believe in that have a unique story, quality, or pricing. As discussed in the previous chapter, this is often called the Unique Selling Proposition (**USP**).

I have never encountered a successful network marketing company that did not have a clear story of their USP. You will want to hear that story.

To remove stress from your business, I suggest that you only consider products that allow you to be your "authentic self". **Would you use or recommend these products even if you did not get paid?** This is another reason most companies have a small purchase requirement every month to remain active. They want their distributors continually enjoying the customer experience.

CONSUMABLE VS. NON-CONSUMABLE

Notice that on both sides of the category list, nearly every product or service is purchased on a regular basis, typically monthly. If the goal is to create long-term residual income, this will be an important factor to consider.

There are successful network marketing companies that sell single-purchase, non-consumable products.

By their nature, single-purchase network marketing companies do not generally build long-term residual income. If residual income is your goal, I recommend sticking with consumable products.

TELLING STORIES

It is often said, "FACTS TELL. STORIES SELL". That is never truer than in network marketing.

Everyone likes to hear inspiring stories of success. As you explore various companies, do your emotions engage when testimonials are given? Do you stay engaged as the "facts" are discussed? You need the facts, you will remember the stories.

Studies show that during person to person communication, people assimilate information in the following order:

50% **visual** or physical

35% **emotion** or excitement

10% words (facts)

5% other

If a distributor is not **visibly excited** about the products or services they promote, they only have a 15% chance of convincing others "this is an idea that can truly make a difference". Do you see yourself sharing success stories about the products you are considering?

In his book, *Street Smart Network Marketing*, Robert Butwin shares a fascinating Japanese concept called "*giri* ". It best translates as *obligation*.

The concept behind it is that once a person has been given something of value and from which they benefit, they are *obligated* to return the favor and give it away to other people.

When we get excited about something, we have a natural reaction to share it with someone else. The greater the benefit we receive from the product or service, the more committed we are to telling others about it.

Think about the countless times you have recommended a movie, a restaurant or a lawn service to a friend. Did the company pay you? Probably not! Have you ever thought they should?

WHERE WILL I FIND CUSTOMERS?

As you consider a product line, and hear the stories of satisfied customers, you should be thinking, "Tamara needs this", "I have to talk to Bob about that", "Tony already uses this every month", "Barbara's kids need this product". If that is not happening, ask for more information or continue your search. You may not see the value in the product line.

You will want to present your new "find" to people you know who would be excited about your discovery, or might know someone who would be. Remember, **85% of the success of a presentation is your own excitement and enthusiasm**.

No enthusiasm, no success!

As much as I love the products, I present the business as my first option, unless there is a specific product interest.

I include an overview of my favorite products in every business presentation and a brief mention of the business in every product presentation. When I finish, if the business is not right for them, I usually am able to sign them as a customer. Simply using this strategy, I have signed up 100's of buying customers over the past 17 years. It works for me. It might work for you, as well.

As you work through the list of people you know, you will begin to expand your network through a variety of methods. Every company has its favorites, and your prospective sponsor will share details about what works best with their specific products.

Speaking of stories, I want to share how a successful stockbroker who fell in love with her company's products went on to create a full-time retirement income. Barb used her company's products for many years before deciding to become a distributor and build her own network marketing business.

IT STARTED WITH THE PRODUCTS

Barb had been a successful stockbroker while raising her family in Florida. As a stockbroker, she had the opportunity to examine every type of business, including the network marketing business model and she knew it worked.

A move across the country to California, where her husband, Sandy, had purchased a specialty window business required the full attention of them both for the first several years. The business was very successful and grew to over 80 Employees, and eventually occupied a 100,000 square foot facility.

However, Barb had become increasingly interested in finding something of her own that she could feel passionate about and create some freedom from her hectic schedule. She proposed to Sandy that she join the network marketing company whose products she knew and trusted.

Over time, she had come to know the leader of the team, and knew he had been enjoying a 6-figure income for many years. **She knew that success was possible.**

Here were her goals:

- Earn a minimum of $100,000/ year
- Be passionate about her work
- Have a business of her own with lifestyle benefits, including flexible hours
- Have the ability to travel – preferably as part of a company rewards program

Sandy agreed, and Barb joined the network marketing company she is still with today.

Barb achieved every one of her initial goals, and so much more. Today she shares her products and business with equal enthusiasm, and is a highly requested speaker and trainer, traveling throughout the US, Canada and Mexico. Her team is growing in several countries, and she enjoys the financial benefits and recognition that her position brings. She has earned over 20 company-paid trips, including Rome, Alaska and Atlantis.

Barb drives a company-provided car and enjoys an annual 6-figure income that rewards her for the passion she brings every time she speaks about the profession she loves.

In the next chapter, we will look at the variety of ways in which you can be paid for your efforts. We will focus on the information you will need to determine if a company can meet your long-term financial goals.

Try not to become a person of success, but rather try to become a person of value.

~ Albert Einstein

CHAPTER 8

COMPENSATIONS PLANS

The compensation plan (also called the "pay plan") of a network marketing company is the program by which a company rewards its distributors for growth activities achieved.

All companies pay more for behavior they want repeated and less for behavior that is of lower importance to their business model.

If you accept this basic principle, it will help you make an educated decision when considering whether a pay plan will meet your personal goals for the future.

There are generally three components to any compensation plan: IMMEDIATE BONUSES, LONG-TERM COMMISSIONS and PERSONAL REWARDS.

IMMEDIATE BONUSES

These bonuses are paid for getting into action quickly or sponsoring new distributors who join with a "Preferred Pack". This can be an influential part of the plan, in that it gives a new distributor the ability to recapture their investment and begin earning immediate income.

However, if recruiting bonuses are the primary manner in which a company rewards you, you may have one or two concerns.

Companies that base their compensation **primarily** on up-front "recruiting" rewards are often the subject of interest by the Federal Trade Commission. The FTC becomes concerned if the total focus of any company is recruiting, rather than the distribution of products or services.

More importantly, if the pay plan is not adequately balanced to include reasonable long-term product volume commissions, you should question whether it will provide you the residual income you may be seeking in retirement. Look for balance.

LONG TERM VOLUME COMMISSIONS

As we discussed earlier, **RESIDUAL INCOME** is common among inventors, singers, writers and actors. They perform an activity one time, and continue to be compensated for their initial efforts after they are no longer directly involved on a day-to-day basis.

This is similar to how residual income works in network marketing. You share products or services with others who believe in them, and become your customers.

If they continue to buy, you will be paid a commission every month in which they make a purchase.

I am not a compensation expert, but you might consider looking for an overall payout of 20% to 35% commission on your **PERSONALLY GENERATED VOLUME**. Many plans begin at a lower rate, and as you move up in rank, you can increase your commission percentage, as well.

You will also recruit distributors and help them get started in their new business. As long as the customers in their network continue to purchase the products, you should receive a commission on the **OVERALL ORGANIZATIONAL VOLUME** that they and their network produce.

Again, I am not a compensation expert. Each company has a basis for their individual plan. But, as a general rule, an overall payout will be between 4% to 14% of total organizational volume. Commissions may start at a lower percentage and increase as a distributor moves up in rank.

A company may offer percentages different than what has been suggested. Look at similar industries or companies marketing similar products. If the numbers align, don't be afraid to move forward.

Commissions set too low in their product sector could be negative for you as a distributor.

Commissions set to high in their product sector could be bad for the company's bottom line or indicate over-priced products. Look for balance.

PERSONAL REWARDS

This can be in the form of additional cash for achievements, but most often will be in the form of trips, car allowances, jewelry, and other non-cash rewards. For many, this is a significant reason to get involved in network marketing. Let's face it, your job may give you a paycheck, but how often do they give you two tickets to Rome, the keys to a brand new car or a four carat diamond ring. Personal Rewards are outward symbols of success, and each network marketing company offers them in some form.

If this is important to you, be sure to find out the additional rewards your prospective company offers and what you would need to accomplish in order to achieve them.

EARNINGS STATEMENT

Most company presentations include a "what if" statement, which is excellent for the imagination, but rarely if ever, does anyone actually achieve the "what ifs".

Many companies will provide, upon request, an Earnings Statement for the prior year. This is a statement of ACTUAL Earnings by distributors, according to RANK in the pay plan. It should be generated from actual 1099 income statements. The purpose is clear. The "what ifs" are great, but show me what actually happens.

Not every company provides these statements. While I would not, automatically, eliminate a company that did not have one, I would do additional research to determine the true potential income at each rank. That information will be far more revealing than the "what if" assumptions.

TYPES OF COMPENSATION PLANS

No two pay plans are exactly alike, so side-by-side comparisons can be difficult. I personally prefer an explanation of:

- What **immediate bonuses** are available and how are they earned"?

- What percent is paid out on **personally generated volume**? How will I qualify?

- What percent is paid out on **total organizational volume**? How will I qualify?

- What **additional rewards** are offered and how are they earned?

- An **Earnings Statement** to determine the overall success of the compensation plan.

While there are only a few defined plans, there are nearly as many hybrid plans as there are companies, so we will only provide an overview. There are four primary compensation plans.

BREAKAWAY

Often called Break-Away or "Stair-Step Break Away". This plan was the "industry standard" for many years and is still widely used today. The plan allows unlimited first level width, with payment to a finite depth (usually 4 to 7 generations).

As a distributor advances in rank, (stair-steps) and others on their team promote in rank, a portion of the volume "BREAKS AWAY" from the upline leader's pay and is added to the emerging leader's compensation. There can be a breakaway of volume or rank qualifications.

MATRIX

Limited first level width (usually 2 -7 positions) and finite depth (usually 5-12 levels). Often described as a "3 x 10" or "4 x 8" matrix. The sponsor places all distributors enrolled beyond the first level width limit deeper in the matrix. This is called spillover.

BINARY

First level width usually limited to two distributors. Commissions are based on the accumulated sales volume in each of the two legs (distributors). The plan is not as much about depth as it is about accumulated volume in each leg.

You are generally paid weekly on the leg with the least volume. Any excess volume is carried over to the next period. However, some binary's "flush" the excess and your work from the prior period is lost. If you are looking at a company with a Binary Plan, I recommend asking a few additional questions. Binaries often allow you to purchase multiple positions in your network, increasing your potential payout, but adding additional expense. If your prospective sponsor recommends this concept, be sure to clarify the total cost before joining.

UNILEVEL

Allows unlimited first level width and finite depth (usually 5-9 levels) with linear commissions. No breakaway occurs, and you may place distributors on any level.

WANT TO KNOW MORE ABOUT PAY PLANS?

There is no good, better, best! If you ask the average distributor, theirs is the BEST!

There are a number of books that go into greater depth on each type of pay plan. If your interest is such that you want to learn more, I suggest *MLM Compensation Pay Plans,* by Rod Cook.

It is important to note that **companies have a clause written into their distributor agreement allowing changes, from time to time, to their compensation plan.**

Reputable companies often create new incentives and rewards that are timelier or have been requested by field leaders. Plans can change to reflect new product incentives or add depth or width to the plan. If you chose a company that has a history of making positive changes to their plan, you should feel comfortable that changes will add benefit to your distributorship, and not negatively affect your income.

I know you will enjoy the next story of how Jody's long-term plan completely changed her future.

PART-TIME RETIREMENT PLAN

Following in her father's footsteps, Jody had reached a pinnacle in her career as the first female Farm and Ranch Appraiser in the state of Idaho. She loved the freedom to be outdoors riding her horse to property surveys, and camping out overnight, often for a week or more, in remote areas of Idaho.

But, there were concerns about constant changes in her industry, including the rising cost of insurance and increasing liability.

Work slowed in the snow-covered winter months, which meant tightly managing money to cover year round expenses such as office space, continuing education and ever-increasing premiums on required insurance coverage. **There was another underlying concern common to many self-employed small business owners, not enough was being put away for retirement.**

An old high school friend called and asked Jody if she could drop by and show her a new business she had just started. It was only out of a desire to be polite that Jody agreed to meet with her. The friend had been involved in a number of network marketing businesses, without much success.

She had invited Jody to try products in the past, but this time was different. The friend brought her sponsor who actually explained the network marketing business model. Jody had never seen the income potential before, and she was intrigued. The concept made perfect sense.

At 38, Jody was enjoying her appraisal work, and never planned on network marketing as a career, but she could see the potential to spend some time, in the slow winter months, beginning to fund her future retirement. She had no intention of quitting the appraisal business at the height of her success, but she did have a wanderlust that included a desire to travel, and eventually move from Idaho to a less severe winter climate.

Her initial goal was to work the program part-time for ten years, and build a residual income of $1,000 per month.

She followed the plan the presenter laid out, and created a list of people she knew who might be looking for the same benefits that had drawn her to the business idea.

Jody was bold! She put state senators and wealthy business people on her list and approached them all. Many became her customers. Others joined the business. She met them over her lunch break each day and with that simple plan, hit her ten year goal of $1,000 per month in her first year. By the third year, her income equaled her appraisal income. Now she had options.

Jody began reducing the time she spent appraising and increasing her concentration on her part-time business, and it paid off. At age 46, eight years after starting her new career, Jody closed the appraisal business, and began living her dream of seeing the country with her husband, Phil.

She continues to support her team online, and by phone wherever she is traveling. Jody loves helping others to achieve their dreams through network marketing, just as she was able to realize her own dream, and so much more.

An unexpected benefit of creating a residual income in her network marketing business was the financial legacy she would leave to those she loves.

Today, at 56, Jody earns a full time income, and has the mobility and freedom she was seeking in retirement. "If I hadn't done network marketing, I would still be living in Idaho, looking for that next appraisal job and probably never have been able to retire."

THE NEXT STEP

Hopefully, you now have an idea of the type of products you want to represent and an idea of what you are looking for in a pay plan. Next, we will look at some helpful tips in selecting a financially stable company that will stand behind their products, and support you, their distributor, now and in the future.

I'd rather attempt to do something great and fail than to attempt to do nothing and succeed.

~ Robert H. Schuller

CHAPTER 9

CHOOSING YOUR CORPORATE PARTNER

It is estimated that over 1,200 different companies, representing 100's of different product categories, use the network marketing method of distribution.

No two are exactly alike. Products differ, compensation plans differ, and company philosophies differ. Reputable network marketing companies are seeking to create value for their customers, their distributors and within the company culture.

Well–intentioned companies, **whether traditional business or network marketing,** experience a similar failure rate of 80% within their first 5 years. Understanding the factors that influence success or failure will provide the information needed to search out a company with the highest potential for long-term success.

Please, do not see this as an indictment of start-up companies. Remember that 20% will succeed. Your goal is to determine if the "success factors" are present.

Imagine you were investing $1,000,000, instead of a few $100, to start a business. You would investigate the background and success of the business idea.

100,000's of people earn 5, 6 and 7-figure incomes in network marketing for a relatively small investment. Your future depends on making a careful selection of a company that fits your needs and interests. Take your time and do not be pressured by statements such as "this opportunity will not last" or "get in on the ground floor". It should not matter whether you sign up today, tomorrow or next week.

This diagram will help explain the relationship between your corporate partner, your sponsorship team and you.

PARTNER RELATIONSHIPS

CORPORATE PARTNER	YOU	SPONSORSHIP TEAM
Products		Training
Branding	Focus	Mentoring
Manufacturing	Ambition	Systems
Distribution	Coach-ability	Strategic Planning
Tracking	Work	Team Support
Compensation		Recognition

Each partner, including you, brings something to the table. If you understand this relationship, it will help you know what to look for and what to expect.

Let's get specific about the "success factors" that will help determine if you have found a qualified Corporate Partner.

This is a pretty thorough list, and there may be additional considerations that are relevant to you. Be sure to take them into account, as well. There is no guarantee of success. But, it is generally in these areas that you will be able to predict whether a company has long-term potential.

Fifteen Things To Look For - A Checklist

1. Length Of Time In Business

This is not an absolute guarantee of future success, nor a predictor of failure, but you will want to consider it as you begin examining potential corporate partners. Many experts consider the five year mark the best predictor of success.

On the other end of the spectrum, consider if length of time in business has made a company "stale". Even successful companies can become complacent. Are they keeping up with current trends, creating new products, expanding into new markets, or are they "stuck in a rut"?

2. Product and Price

Are customers buying the product enthusiastically based, on its own merit, even if they do not participate in the compensation program?

Is it a high quality or unique product for which there is a strong demand in the "real-world" market?

Are they priced competitively with **similar quality** products? Can the product be demonstrated, and will it "stand out" when shown to friends? Is the product patented or proprietary to the company and available only through its distributors? Are the products consumable? Remember that in order to generate true residual income, products must be purchased continually, on a regular basis.

Are the products backed by a customer satisfaction guarantee or a money-back guarantee? Is post-sales service or customer assistance available from the company?

3. No Large Investment Requirement

Can you become a distributor without having to fulfill a large inventory requirement? Immediate internet access to products, and the availability of overnight delivery has made stocking inventory in your garage a thing of the past.

Complete business kits typically range from $299 to $1000. If finances allow the purchase of a complete Distributor Kit, I recommend it. Consider asking for information on ALL options available to join.

If someone decides not to follow through as a distributor, is there a buy-back program on the kit and unused product purchases?

There will most likely, be a small monthly fee for a company created website. Ask about any additional ongoing monthly expense.

4. Sales Commissions Sources

Sales commissions should be paid on actual products or services sold by a distributor, to an end-user within their network.

Does the pay plan avoid paying commissions or bonuses for the sole act of recruiting new distributors? Bonuses paid solely for recruiting, without the movement of some product, could become the subject of interest to the FTC, SEC, and other government agencies.

5. Presentation and Training Tools

While distributors often use tools provided by their sponsor, most companies provide basic presentation websites, online sign up, and "getting started" training. Are these tools available from the company?

If there are questions about the ability to use the tools provided, consider attending an event and observing the process.

6. Back Office

Does the company provide a system of accounting for your personal customers, distributors, and the customers and distributors in your network? Can a distributor track daily and monthly activity, and monitor anticipated commission payments? Is there an additional cost for these services?

Does the company maintain regular customer contact or is that up to the distributor? Do they provide a basic contact management system?

7. Company Direct

Do customers **BUY DIRECT** from the company through your personal website, mobile app or an 800 number? Busy people today expect these methods of shopping and paying online.

Are physical products **SHIPPED DIRECT** from the company to the customer? Are refunds and exchanges handled by the company? You should expect a commission chargeback when a refund is issued by the company.

Are commissions and bonuses **PAID DIRECT** from the company? How often are they paid? Do they offer Direct Deposit?

8. Earnings Representation

Does the company's literature and training materials scrupulously avoid promises of specific incomes, other than providing demonstrations of verifiable income levels within its program? For instance, a company should have statistics (Earnings Statements) to show the actual incomes, realized by the average distributor, at each rank.

9. Will-able and Sale-able

As your business grows, you will want to know that in the event something happens to you, your business would pass to your spouse, partner or heirs.

Better yet, will it be a legacy for your children and their children as we have shown in many of the stories included in this book?

Do not take this for granted. Some companies have forced retirement programs, as young as 65 years old. You will want to know this, in advance, if you are looking for long-term retirement income.

There will most likely be paperwork to file with the company designating your intentions. Failure to file the paperwork could block your wishes from being carried out. If this is of significant importance to you, find out the process to take these actions.

10.   Orphan Commissions

When a distributor fails to qualify to earn the commissions or bonuses on their volume in any given month (usually because they fall short of the minimum purchase qualifying amount), the commissions they would have earned are referred to as "orphan" commissions.

A pay plan should be structured in such a way that orphan commissions "roll up" to the next qualifying distributor rather than being retained by the company. This roll-up is also referred to as "compression".

Orphan commissions from terminated distributors should be handled in the same way.

11. Financial Stability

More companies fail for this reason than any other. What is their financial backing? Rapid growth is expensive, and a company that starts out in debt will have an uphill battle.

Is the company debt-free? This may not be easily determined for a non-publically traded company. However, when a company is debt-free, distributors are usually familiar with that fact and proudly share it.

The benefit of publically traded vs. privately held ownership has been debated among distributors, as to whether it adds value or is a hindrance to growth. Many long-time companies in which a founder has retired or died have become publically traded, but the majority of network marketing companies are privately held.

There are many successful companies in both categories and I have not found it a predictor of success or failure. Public or private, you should be able to find details about the ownership and financial stability of the company.

12. Experience Of Management Team

They may produce a good product, but does the management team have experience in running a network marketing company, compensation plan structure, manufacturing and marketing?

Often the corporate website will provide background and expertise of the senior management team. Do they have clear goals for future expansion of both products and international markets?

13.   Training & Distributor Support

Does the company offer its independent distributors solid training in both product sales and recruitment?

Are different levels of training offered to match the increasing level of experience and responsibilities of distributors?

14.   Reputation

If you are not satisfied with the information you have received, or even if you are, you may want to take some time to check with organizations such as the Direct Sellers Association, the Better Business Bureau or simply "Google" the company and watch the online conversation. Remember, not everything on the internet is factual. Be sure to investigate further before accepting negative information, particularly if it is found on the internet.

15.   Sense Of FUN And Excitement

You will hopefully be spending the rest of your network marketing career with this company, and your team. They will become some of your dearest friends. Are they fun to be around? Are company events interesting and full of action? If this aspect is important to you, consider attending an event and seeing for yourself.

Whew! That was an exhausting list. Remember, **NO company will ever answer every question perfectly**. Make sure that your key considerations have been answered satisfactorily.

Here's another success story that will encourage you that pursuing a network marketing career can result in the outcome you are seeking. Invest the time, and you will find a company that can provide the benefits you are looking for.

A DESIRE TO BE HOME WITH HER KIDS

At the age of 34, Renee, her husband David, and their three young sons had recently moved to California from Minnesota.

For years, she had worked in a family business where she often felt the in-equality of pay as family members who worked little, and showed up less, received the same pay, though Renee worked a 60 to 70 hour week and often had to travel representing the business. She promised herself that if she ever took another job, she would be paid what she was worth, based on her own efforts.

Her true goal was to stay home with her three sons, but the family budget required that she generate some income, as well.

Renee and David calculated the gross income that a new job would bring. Then they deducted the savings that could be realized by working from home. No daycare. No dry cleaning. No expensive lunches. No commute or auto expense. After deducting all the potential cost savings, they figured that she would need to bring home only $800 per month, and they would be even.

About that time, a friend invited her to a small meeting in a local hotel to hear about a business idea.

Renee had never heard the term "network marketing" before, but as the speaker outlined the benefits of owning your own business, getting paid what you are worth (sound familiar), and the time freedom that working from home could provide, she realized immediately that this was just what she was looking for.

The idea of being compensated for the volume you personally produce for a company, and being rewarded when your team produces volume, just made sense.

Network marketing was a mind-shift for Renee in the beginning. She had always worked Business to Business, so it took a while to make the transition to People to People. Eventually, she became passionate, not only about the products her company marketed, but that she was able to help other young moms stay home with their kids, as well.

As the business grew, BOTH Renee and David were able to be stay-at-home parents and raise their three sons together, never missing a sporting or school event that involved their kids. Renee consistently meets her monthly financial goal and has enjoyed a full-time annual income in her network marketing business for the past 15 years.

Probably the biggest "Ah Ha" moment of her career came in 2007 when her home and all her belongings were lost in the San Diego fires. It took three years to straighten out the legal, zoning and government regulations to re-build her home.

Her commission checks arrived each month, even though she was unable to work her business for nearly three years. Renee calls her network marketing income true "mailbox money". Although she no longer had a mailbox, her checks were direct-deposited to her bank account every month.

The boys are now in college, and she is transitioning her business from a household budget income into a retirement savings fund for her future.

Renee has no plan to retire anytime soon. In her own words, "When you find something you love to do, and you can still do it, it isn't really work, is it?"

ALMOST DONE WITH THE DETAILS

So far, we have examined criteria for Products, Compensation Plans and your Corporate Partner. There is one more search that you will want to complete, and that is to make sure you have the right business partner, **your sponsor**.

Success in this industry is not in finding the right person, but in becoming the right person.

~Dr. Forrest Shaklee

CHAPTER 10

INTERVIEWING POTENTIAL SPONSORS

Recently, I was sitting in a conference and heard the speaker, make the following comment about the **silent agreement** between a sponsor and their distributor when the sponsor does not have a clear process. **"I will pretend to teach you, if you will pretend to learn"**. It struck me like an arrow.

How many times had someone who previously joined a network marketing company and became discouraged, say to me "I was excited about the products and the company, but I did not know what to do, so I quit"?

Let me be clear; this is **NOT about the experience of your sponsor**. It is NOT about how long they have been in their respective company. It is NOT about how much money they are making.

It IS about their ability to provide a clear process that a new distributor can follow from the day they join, which will, in turn, duplicate in their own team as they build toward their own success.

NO PROCESS, NO SUCCESS!

You could "re-invent the wheel" and come up with your own process, but that will put you out of sync with the rest of your team, and that is not the goal. Instead, you want to put your sponsor to work for you, while you learn the team process.

When our team was looking to join a new company, we decided as a group what we would be looking for in selecting a sponsor. The questions below will help in formulating that initial interview.

Again, let me make it clear, **your friend who just joined a company last week is the perfect sponsor, if they, or their upline leader can answer your questions about the help and support they will provide.** Rest assured, that if your sponsor is receiving the needed support, you will, as well. That would make them a qualified sponsor. It is not about time in the business; it is about a process designed for success.

Throughout this book, I have not referred to commonly used terms such as "upline" or "downline." I much prefer "business partner" or "team member". However, in this case, I am referring to a relationship placement, and need to explain a simple concept.

When I was a real estate broker, there was a cardinal rule in my office. Never tell anyone (including other agents in my own office) what I am doing or how I am doing it. Similar requirements are found in other professions, as well. When I joined network marketing, I soon realized that I did not have to guard my secrets, but, in fact, needed to give "my best stuff" to everyone on the team. It was amazing to find a business where the success of the individual members benefit the whole team. What a concept!

Once you realize this, you will understand that you are never "bugging" a leader who is upline from you. True leaders are searching for people on the team they can help and support. Your success flows up to them.

PLAN YOUR SPONSOR INTERVIEW

Select pertinent questions from the list below. The more serious you are about building a business, the more questions you should ask. If your prospective sponsor is new, consider asking them to include a more experienced upline in the discussion.

Since your prospective sponsor may have never been asked these questions in the past, do not hesitate to give them your list in advance. It could save you both a lot of time.

Here are some questions to consider:

What are your goals?

Are you on track to achieve them?

What hours are you typically available to help me?

What has been your product experience so far?

How many product users have you signed up?

How do you present the products? Ask them for a demonstration if you have not seen one previously.

How many distributors have you sponsored? None is not always a negative answer. Ask them to explain.

How do you present the business opportunity? Ask them for a demonstration if you have not seen one previously.

Are there online product and business presentations?

Are there local events? When and where?

Who is your direct upline leader? How long have they been in the business? **You might consider asking to be introduced.** Are they available to support you?

Who is the top leader of the team? Ask for their business story. Are they available to support you?

Are there conference calls that I can plug into?

Are training materials located online or offline? (This will be important if you live in Seattle and recruit your cousin in New Jersey)

Is there a team website (apart from the corporate website) with team training and tools available?

Is there a clear process to get started? Would you briefly explain it?

Ask, "If I were to get started today, what would I be doing?"

How will you help me?

Will I be able to use the same process for my new distributors?

If you plan to market ONLINE, you need to ask some questions regarding training on social media tools and the **company policy regarding online marketing**. Some companies have very restrictive internet policies while others do not police any online activity. Both of these can be negative to an online marketer. Be sure to request the social media policy of the company and check out a few distributors who are marketing online. You will get a good sense of what is permitted.

As you read Chapter 11, you will see how the answers to these questions fit into the discussion on the skills of a network marketing professional.

Before we get to that, I'd like to introduce my friend, Jan, who is a top sponsor in her company.

A MASTER NETWORKER

Jan knew early on that she would be a success. She had grown up in a 900 sq. ft. home with 7 children, and determined that she would create a successful career for herself and her future family. Her life would be different.

Following the traditional route, she went to college and earned her Master's Degree in Business. She was hired by IBM Corporation and eventually became the CFO of a major division of the company.

After 19 years, she realized that although she had what would be classified as a "good retirement plan", it would eventually require a significant drop in lifestyle. She was not interested in making that transition.

A friend invited her to look at a part-time business that would allow her to build additional retirement income in her "spare time". After she finished laughing at the idea of actually having spare time, Jan said, "what the heck" and decided to give it a try.

Given a project or task, Jan approaches everything with enthusiasm. Network marketing was no exception. But, even she was surprised to find that after only one year, her "part time" income matched her corporate salary.

Excited, but not totally confident that her new business success would continue, she took a leave of absence from IBM to see what could happen if she put her full effort into building her network marketing income.

It was not long before Jan was earning a 5-figure (and often a 6–figure) income per month. She became one of the top earners in her company, which had over 2,000,000 Distributors. Needless to say, she never considered returning to the long days and stress of corporate life.

For the past 16 years, Jan has worked from her home in Colorado. She believes her calling is "leading others to success". Jan's passion to help others, has led to the creation of a highly successful network marketing career which has secured her future retirement.

When that day arrives, it will not require a lifestyle change. After all, that was her original goal.

IS IT BEGINNING TO COME TOGETHER?

We have gone through the process of determining product interest, and understanding the basic elements of a pay plan. We have detailed 15 important considerations when choosing a company, and have created a list of questions to determine the qualifications of a potential sponsor.

It is time to take a closer look at the skills we have been discussing throughout each chapter .

What would you be doing?

What skills do you have already?

What skills will you need to learn?

Being a professional is doing the things you love to do, including on the days you don't feel like doing them

~Julius Irving

CHAPTER 11

THE SKILLS YOU WILL LEARN

Like any new business owner, there are skills you will need to learn, or improve, in order to achieve success. It's NOT about your personality, your looks, where you were born, your family, or your background. It's about your skill set.

Developing each of these skills will increase your value and your income. The good news is that **improving each of these skills will prove valuable in EVERY area of life**. You will want to develop in three major areas.

PEOPLE SKILLS

People are everywhere! You work with them, live with them, buy things from them, and sell things to them. Where does money come from? People! If you learn more about people than you do anything else, you will be unusually successful. If you develop great people skills, you can achieve income security.

PROFESSIONAL SKILLS

Whether you are a doctor, real estate agent, mechanic, waitress, teacher, home business owner, or customer service rep, you must know the basics of your profession. You need to be willing to learn new, specialized skills. The difference between a professional and an amateur is their skill level.

LEADERSHIP SKILLS

People with strong leadership skills have high influence and value in the marketplace. They consistently work on improving themselves as they raise up other leaders. They have a "no excuses" mindset. They focus on producing results. They do not let circumstances define their success, but they take personal responsibility to create their own success.

If you continue to do the same things you have always done, you will continue to get the same results you have always gotten.

Take your skills to the next level. If you want to succeed, you will need to master: people skills, professional skills and leadership skills.

There are **SEVEN SPECIFIC SKILLS** you will develop or improve throughout your network marketing career. As you learn to apply each skill, it will become part of your "authentic self", and you will soon practice it effortlessly as you go about building a successful network.

SKILL 1. FIND AND CONNECT WITH PEOPLE

There are only 2 kinds of people:

- Those you already know

- Those you will meet

The skill is connecting with each group and learning how to uncover a need that your products, services or business opportunity might satisfy. It is important to understand that **no matter what business you are in, not everyone will be interested**. Your goal is to communicate your offer and let them decide if it is right for them.

People you already know are often referred to as your WARM NETWORK. This group includes family, friends, neighbors, owners and employees of small businesses you frequent, and business connections from your present or past networks that would recognize you by name.

The most important thing to understand is that YOU DON'T HAVE to ask any of them to purchase your product or join your business.

But, you do need to tell them about your new business, and simply ask for their support.

BE HONEST WITH YOURSELF

Let's say you opened a coffee shop on the next corner. Would you keep it a secret from your family and friends? Of course not!

You would tell everyone you know, about your new venture, invite them to your Grand Opening and ask them to tell their friends. Some will come, some don't drink coffee. That's okay! They now know about your business, and where you are located. Even if they don't come, they are likely to tell their coffee drinking friends about your new venture. You would invite them to attend, whether they would show up or not.

The people you don't know yet are often referred to as your COLD MARKET, and there are literally BILLIONS of them. Like any business owner, you can attend local meet-ups, networking groups, join clubs, etc. and extend your outreach daily. Most professionals set a goal to meet 1-3 new people every day and add them to their network. You will create your own plan for when, where, and how you will begin making those connections.

If you followed this process of adding 1-3 new people to your contact manager every day, you would create 300 to 1,000 new contacts every year.

- Make note, in your Contact Manager where you met them, and their business or personal interests. Calendar a follow up time.

- Determine something you could do to **benefit them** and further the connection.

- Send them a "nice to meet you" card or e-mail. Make a phone call, send them a referral, or invite them to coffee.

- Stay in touch.

At some point, you will have the opportunity to ask them to look at your business, products, or provide referrals. Always remember, it is a two-way street.

SKILL 2. INVITE THEM TO LEARN MORE

It is important to understand that success in this second skill requires you to use tools provided by the company or your team leader.

Invite people to attend a team webinar, listen to a CD or view an online video. Give them a DVD or a catalog. Ask for their e-mail address to send information about a specific interest.

Always keep in mind one simple principle of network marketing. Every time you speak, you are training that person on exactly what they would be doing if they joined you. If you are a skilled salesperson and rely on your personality to get people to respond, you will not be able to duplicate that within your team.

So, do and teach what ANYONE can do.

FOUR SIMPLE WORDS have been extremely effective in the invitation process. Anyone can learn four words.

IF I.....WOULD YOU?

Let me give you a couple of simple examples:

Product: "Mary, I think I might have a solution for that problem. **IF I** gave you a CD which specifically addresses your concern, **WOULD YOU** listen to it?"

<u>Service:</u> "Bill, I found a company that has really helped me with that issue. **IF I** sent you a website address, **WOULD YOU** have time to look at it?"

<u>Business:</u> "Susan, I am part of a company that is helping people earn extra income working part time, from home. I have planned a small gathering at my house on Wednesday at 7:00. **IF I** invited you, **WOULD YOU** be able to make it?"

If the answer is "yes", confirm the information, and follow up as promised. If the answer is "no", thank them for their time, offer them a business card and ask, "Do you know someone who might be interested in the products or wants to earn extra income."

The book I will refer to you will provide details of the three types of people you will invite, and a script that you can learn for each one. I strongly recommend making that purchase if you decide to become a network marketing professional.

SKILL 3. PRESENTING the INFORMATION

The most important concept you will need to grasp about this third skill is that you are the MESSENGER, not the MESSAGE. Your role is to deliver the tool with enthusiasm.

How you do this is critical. Can they see themselves doing what you did? If you complicate your presentation, they will see your business or products as complicated. Their reaction will be, "I CAN'T IMAGINE DOING THAT". That is not the response you are looking to hear.

If you keep it simple and use the available tools, you will hear them say, **"I COULD DO THAT"**.

If they don't say, "NO" but they don't say, "YES" to either the products or the business idea following the presentation, the next skill will prove invaluable.

SKILL 4. FOLLOW UP

People generally make product purchase decisions "on the spot" or fairly soon after a presentation. If they did not, usually a quick phone call or personal visit will be sufficient to get their response.

A decision to join you in your business may take longer. It is not always about money. They may have unanswered questions about the business (see Chapter 6) or concerns about making the time commitment.

It may take one, two, seven or eight follow-up contacts for you to get a YES or a NO. **Anything in between is a MAYBE.**

In my own case, it took about ten contacts before I watched the recorded presentation. What if my friends had stopped at three or even eight follow up calls? I assure you, that video cassette would have eventually made it to the trash and my life would be sadly different today. **I am grateful for their follow up.**

In this social media and e-mail world, there is a strong temptation to let these tools do the work for us. While they are valid forms of staying in touch and connecting with people, there is no substitute for a phone call or personal visit.

An e-mail cannot judge their response, answer questions they might have, or encourage them to, "Just watch it for me, and I promise I won't bother you about it further if you're not interested".

Each time you make a connection, it is important to set up the next contact. "Okay, I understand that you haven't had a chance to look at the information, do you think you could check it out in the next couple of days?" Get their response. "Okay, I'll call you back on Friday".

SKILL 5. ASKING THEM TO JOIN YOU

If you have followed the process described above, it is a natural "next step" to invite the person to join you as a customer or distributor.

Are you prepared at each contact for a "YES"? Do you have sign-up forms or online access for those product customers interested in joining you? If so, simply let them know that you have the information available for them to place their order today. Explain the sign up process and provide the link or form. Let them know you will be happy to help them fill it out.

There are a few additional questions you will want to ask potential distributors who may decide to join you. You will learn a simple six question process as you develop this skill.

Unless you get a firm NO, you should never leave an appointment without setting a time or circumstance for the next follow up. If you don't do this, you will struggle with, "Is it too early to call them?" or worse, "Have I waited too long?" Setting that next appointment lets you both know what to expect.

Some will say YES, some will say NO. Others will stay in the MAYBE column for a while. Continue to follow up and allow them to go through their own process and you are on the right track.

SKILL 6. GET THEM STARTED RIGHT

A new distributor is excited. They have invested time and money to start their own business. They are anxious to get into action.

Immediately after you sign up a new distributor, do two things:

1. Provide them a **"Getting Started" Document** with simple assignments they can begin today.

2. Set an appointment for their **One Hour Initial Strategy Session**, which should be completed within 1-2 days of their joining.

One step in the Getting Started process should be to order the book, ***Go Pro*, by Eric Worre**. We have referred to it throughout this chapter. The book goes into great depths on each of the **seven skills**. Information to purchase that book can be found in the Appendix. Make it part of your toolbox and encourage every distributor to read it several times.

Remember, in network marketing you will be paid to do only three things:

1. **Use the products**

2. **Present the products and business**

3. **Teach your team to do 1 and 2**

Since these three simple things are what you will be **paid** to do. You will want to spend 80% of your time doing them. Mastering the seven skills will help you accomplish each step in a professional manner, with confidence.

Yes, there are other aspects of the business that a leader will learn as they move forward, but if we start new distributors doing money-making activities right away, they will earn their first check, and their belief level will soar.

SKILL 7. GETTING PEOPLE TO SHOW UP

You now have a brief summary of the first six skills. You will need to develop each one, but **your success depends on the seventh and final skill**, getting people to show up.

It can be frustrating to lose an hour of your day because you went to the coffee shop for an appointment, and no one showed up. Or, you planned an event at your home; six people confirmed, and only two showed up. It happens!

Don't take it personally. It has less to do with you and your opportunity than it does with life or circumstances getting in the way.

However, **there is a skill in getting people to show up to your events**. You will learn the complete process in the *Go Pro* book. Over time, you will perfect this process and it will greatly increase your success.

KNOWN FOR HIS SKILLS

Gary is an unusual guy. Quiet and reserved, you would never guess that he headed a team which produces over 8,000,000 in annual volume, for his network marketing company.

With a background as a high school football coach, Gary understands the concept of inspiring people to take action, and teaching the fundamentals of success.

At the age of 31, Gary was meeting with an insurance agent planning his future needs, when the discussion led to making money.

The Agent was not in network marketing himself, but said **he knew a guy who was "looking for people who wanted to make some extra income".**

Gary said he was "not interested", but asked for the man's information anyway. A few days later, he found himself sitting in the man's living room, learning about a way to make money by sharing products and an earnings opportunity with interested people.

The presentation consisted of a simple product demonstration, stories of people who were achieving success, and describing what Gary would be doing if he wanted to earn money, as well. The most memorable part of the evening for Gary, was the conversation about "building something" that could create a long-term income for his future. That was just what he was seeking. He paid the $4.50 distributor fee that night, and he was in business.

Faye, Gary's wife, wasn't quite as excited about his new business, but she became very supportive as Gary forged ahead. He was making it work by being consistent with his thinking and efforts. He had a vision for the legacy they could create for the benefit of others and their own future family.

Looking back on that evening, in the man's living room, Gary comments on two parts of the presentation that made an impression he carried into the future.

First, "The guy never told me how good this idea really was. In fact, it turned out far better than I could have ever imagined".

Second**, when Gary committed to doing everything the** guy said, which was to **find two people each year for the next five years who wanted to earn some extra income,** he wished the guy would have said three people per year. "I can't imagine what would have happened if I had done that."

Here are a few of Gary's thoughts about network marketing:

- It's not about personality
- It's about doing what you need to do to make an income for the future of you and your family
- It's about having the time freedom and quality of life that network marketing can provide anyone who is willing to follow a plan
- Don't listen to those who have NOT done it.
- Listen to the Leaders on your team who HAVE done it.

Today at 75, Gary and Faye live a life that even they could not have dreamed. Spending time at their home in Minneapolis, summers at their lake home and winters in Phoenix, where they can golf every day, was not something they could have imagined when they began this journey 43 years ago.

With lifetime earnings in excess of $12 Million, it is not simply about money anymore. Gary and Faye continue to work their business daily, inspiring others and encouraging them that anyone can achieve their dreams, if they are willing to put in the time and effort.

Oh, by the way. Gary did change one fundamental teaching. He now teaches that you should find THREE leaders every year for five years, not TWO.

STORIES MAKE IT REAL

Here is one last story of success. It's another multi-generational network marketing business that is making a difference in the lives of many.

FROM A TOWN OF 2,000

Mary was on her way back to her hometown of Meridian, Idaho, population 2,000 at the time, and stopped for a visit at the home of a friend. The friend was insistent that Mary try a product she was sure would prove valuable on the farm that Mary operated with her husband, Austin.

The year was 1960, and the beginning of a **legacy network marketing business** now operated by Mary's daughter Linda and her husband Reed.

Linda had become a distributor in the business upon turning 18, but college, marriage and motherhood were her primary focus in those early years.

Reed began a traditional career by earning his Master's Degree and becoming a college teacher, while Linda stayed home with their growing family.

In 1972, faced with a contract renewal of his teaching position, Reed discussed his future with a number of other teachers at the college and was dismayed at the long-term outlook. Many felt that they would never receive a return on the investment in their education, even after a lifetime of teaching.

Meanwhile, Mary was successfully building her business simply sharing the products and the business, just as her friend had shared with her.

By 1972, she was earning three to four times her son-in-law's annual salary as a college teacher. She was driving a new company-provided car every 2 years, and earning international trips, also paid for by the company. It was not difficult, for Reed to reach the decision to join Mary in her business, rather than renew his teaching contract.

Linda and Reed took over the active management of the business, and it grew steadily. In 1996, they purchased Mary's interest in the business, which today produces over 7,000,000 in volume monthly for their company, and has allowed them to live a life that would never have been possible on a teacher's salary or pension. The purchase of Mary's interest in the business provided a benefit for her extended family, as well.

Today, at 67 and 70, respectively, Linda and Reed are enjoying the benefits that a $400,000+ annual retirement income affords. They are training their son, Todd, to manage the business as a third generation network marketer. But, it is clear that they are having too much fun to retire just yet. They love helping people and teaching and training young distributors the skills they learned when they were getting started themselves.

Reed had one piece of advice for anyone beginning a career in network marketing. "Don't judge anyone. You have no idea who will be successful. Work with anyone with a strong desire for a different life."

NOW IT'S TIME TO TAKE THE TEST

Let's put what you have learned into determining whether the business might be a good fit for you. Take the simple 20 question quiz. We'll analyze the results after you total your score.

Success is liking yourself, liking what you do, and liking how you do it.

~ Maya Angelou

CHAPTER 12

TIME TO TAKE THE TEST

Let's summarize:
You've discovered your personal Retirement Gap.

You understand the lifestyle and benefits that network marketing can provide.

Hopefully, you got answers to a few nagging questions.

You have a basic understanding of the process you would go through to find the right company, products, pay plan and sponsor.

You know the basic skills you will develop in order to succeed in network marketing.

You're still with me, so you are either curious or interested. That's good!

It's time to take the test to see if network marketing might be a good fit for you.

There are <u>20 questions</u> with a total of <u>200 possible points</u>. Total the points when you have finished.

Each answer should be scored from 1 to 10.

1 = "NO" to   10 = "YES"

If your answer is neutral, rate it from 4 to 6.

_____ 1. Do you enjoy meeting new people?

_____ 2. When you encounter someone with a problem, do you offer solutions or referrals?

_____ 3. Do you enjoy teaching others what you have learned in life or in business?

_____ 4. Have you or someone you know used products sold through network marketing? (Tupperware, Mary Kay, Pampered Chef, etc.)

_____ 5. Do you know someone who has had any level of financial success in network marketing?

_____ 6. Does your current retirement plan have a Gap (1 = small gap, 10 = big gap)

_____ 7. Would you be willing to invest 5-10 hours per week if you could increase your income by $1,000 - $2,000 per month over time?

_____ 8. Do you have concerns about a current or potential health issues that could impact your ability to work in the future?

_____ 9. Have you considered the legacy you will leave your family, and wish you could do more?

_____ 10. Have you ever desired to own your own business?

_____ 11. If I gave you 10 minutes, could you list 10 people who would support you in a business?

_____ 12. Do you know two people who are looking to improve their financial future or want to own their own business?

_____ 13. Do you enjoy being recognized for your achievements?

_____ 14. Do you enjoy travel and wish you could do more?

_____ 15. Would a new car benefit you or someone in your family?

_____ 16. Do you identify with a few of the real people whose stories are told at the end of each chapter?

_____ 17. Rate your general impression of Network Marketing PRODUCTS (1 = poor, 10 = great)

_____ 18. What is your general impression of NWM DISTRIBUTORS? (1 = poor, 10 = great)

_____ 19. Have you already developed some of the seven skills of a professional network marketer?

_____ 20. Are you willing to learn the skills you may currently lack?

_____ ADD UP THE **TOTAL** OF ALL 20 QUESTIONS AND ENTER IT HERE

THE RESULT

While the purpose of this exercise is to cause you to consider your own personal situation, and uncover your inner thoughts or misconceptions about network marketing, the following would be a fairly strong predictor of success.

Whatever your score, feel free to challenge the averages and prove me wrong. The most unlikely people regularly succeed because the only real predictor of success is an unwavering desire for a different future.

If the total is less than 50, my guess is you took the test before finishing the book. Smile! Consider going back to the beginning and taking a "do over". If this is your real score, I suggest you look into extending your current employment.

If your total is between 51 and 100, and you have the drive, will, and emotion to succeed, you are a candidate. You will need a strong support team to overcome some obstacles. You will want to begin working on the seven skills, right away.

If your total score is between 101 and 150, don't hesitate to get back to the person, who gave you this book, you are an excellent candidate for success in network marketing. Many top-earners who took the test scored in this category.

If you scored over 151, you possess the skill and drive to succeed in network marketing. You would be an asset to any team or company. I encourage you to get back to the person who gave you this book.

People often join network marketing for the money, but they stay for the relationships they make with positive energetic forward-thinking people who are pursuing their dreams and goals.

Network marketing will be worth it for:

The people you will meet,

The lives you will change,

The experiences you will have,

The skills you will learn,

The person you will become.

IF NOT NETWORK MARKETING.....WHAT?

IF NOT NOW.....WHEN?

"If you are a person with big dreams and would love to support others in achieving their big dreams, then the network marketing business is definitely a business for you. You can start part-time at first and then as your business grows, you can help other people start their part-time business. This is a value worth having – a business and people who help others make their dreams come true."*

Robert Kiyosaki

Author, *Rich Dad, Poor Dad*

ABOUT THE AUTHOR

Kathi Minsky has been a successful Network Marketer for the past 17 years and is considered *"one of the 52 brightest minds in network marketing"*.
It's Time For Network Marketing, pub. 2007.

At the age of 49, health issues forced her to leave a successful real estate career. Three years earlier, she had begun a part-time network marketing business that was producing a residual income check every month. It caused her to consider the possibility that this could be an option for her future. Within 12 months, she was producing a 6-figure income working part–time while re-gaining her health.

Kathi is a best-selling author, a recognized speaker and trainer, and has received numerous professional awards including Trainer of the Year, Perseverance Award, Circle of Excellence and is the only recipient of her companies Innovator Award for excellence in training and innovation. She has spoken before audiences of 5,000 - 10,000 and has trained 100,000's of Distributors in several countries.

She currently holds the record for achieving her company's top position in just 3 months, sponsoring over 1,400 new distributors in 58 days.

She was one of the first network marketers to "crack the code" of building a successful online business from her home in Fairbanks, Alaska.

Today, Kathi shares her home in sunny Las Vegas with her husband Mike, and 3 cats, Rascal, Sarge and Shy.

ACKNOWLEDGMENTS

To those who shared your stories and thoughts, you are an inspiration to so many.

Gary and Faye Burke, Kay and Bob Ferguson, John Milton Fogg, Reed and Linda Hanson, Barb Hill Behar, Jan Johnson, Rod Larkin, Jody Newell, Jane Pederson, Robin Reves-May, George Shaw, Lorraine Ulrich and Renee Van Heel

Thanks to my personal support team:

Karin Dejan, Denise Folkerts, Claudia Greenleaf, Doug Goudie, John and Jeanie Watkins, Geoff White and Barbara Baum, Claire and John Woodruff and   Virginia Wright

Thanks for your time and support.

Disclaimer

This book is designed to provide information to our readers. It is provided with the understanding that the author and publisher are not engaged to render any type of legal or any other kind of professional advice. The content of each book is the sole expression and opinion of its author, and not necessarily that of the publisher. No warranties or guarantees are expressed or implied as a result of the publisher's choice to include any of the content in this volume. Neither the publisher nor the individual author shall be liable for any damages, including, but not limited to, special, incidental, consequential or other damages.

Our views and rights are the same: You are responsible for your own choices, actions, and results. Please see a legal professional for counsel.

Appendix A

Suggested Books on Network Marketing

GO PRO - 7 Steps To Becoming A NWM Professional
Eric Worre

The Greatest Networker In The World
John Milton Fogg

The Business of the 21st Century
Robert T. Kiyosaki

The Business School For People Who Like Helping People
Robert Kiyosaki and Sharon Lechter

Resources
United States Department of Labor
Taking the Mystery Out of Retirement Planning
62 Page Planning Guide

http://www.dol.gov/ebsa/publications/nearretirement.html

Social Security – Monitor your personal account

www.ssa.gov/myaccount

Statistics

Most of the statistics referenced in this book are obtained from the Direct Sellers Association (DSA)

www.dsa.org/

Made in the USA
Lexington, KY
25 October 2013